THE TIME OF YOUR LIFE!

RITUALS & BELIEFS

Ina Taylor

Hodder & Stoughton

A MEMBER OF THE HODDER HEADLINE GROUP

The Publishers would like to thank the following for permission to reproduce material in this volume:
Extracts from 'The Marriage Service' from The Alternative Service Book 1980 are copyright © The Archbishops' Council of the Church of England and are reproduced by permission; Extracts from Common Worship: Initiation Services (Church House Publishing, 1998) are copyright © The Archbishop's Council of the Church of England and are reproduced by permission; Scriptures quoted from the Good News Bible published by The Bible Societies/Harper Collins Publishers Ltd., UK, © American Bible Society, 1966, 1971, 1976, 1992; Extracts from Funerals without God by Jane Wynne Willson © British Humanist Association 1989 and Sharing the Future by Jane Wynne Willson © British Humanist Association 1988, 1996; The Catholic Truth Society for the extract from the Roman Catholic Marriage Service; ENGINEERS of the IMAGINATION for the 'Lorry Driver's Funeral', p.163 from THE DEAD GOOD FUNERALS BOOK by Sue Gill and John Fox 1996, reprinted 1997; Penguin Books for the extracts from The Koran with Parallel Text, translated by NJ Dawood, 1995.

The Publishers would like to thank the following for permission to reproduce the following copyright illustrations in this volume:
Christine Osborne Pictures p9, 12, 15, 31, 61, 62, 64; Circa Photo Library p13, (Barry Searle) 27, (B J Mistry) 30; Corbis p55, 79; Phil Emmett p11, 24, 28, 45, 60, 67, 73; Will Lack p56; Life File p66, (Nigel Suttleworth) 4, 36, (Graham Burns) p5, (Richard Powers) 65; The photos on pages 10 and 39 are reproduced with the kind permission of Manchester Jewish Museum; News Team, Birmingham/Paul Rogers p49; PA News/David Jones p69; PA Photos/Barry Batchelor p48; Science Photo Library p74; Somerset Willow Company p68; Tate Gallery Publications p70; Ina Taylor p8, 10, 15, 16, 18, 19, 33, 39, 40, 41, 44, 46, 47 (both), 58, 59, 78; The Walking Camera (Alex Keene) p25;

Every effort has been made to trace and acknowledge copyright. The publishers will be happy to make suitable arrangements with any copyright holder whom it has not been possible to contact.

Orders: please contact Bookpoint Ltd, 130 Milton Park, Abingdon, Oxon OX14 48B. Telephone: (44) 01235 827720, Fax: (44) 01235 400454. Lines are open from 9.00 - 6.00, Monday to Saturday, with a 24 hour message answering service. Email address: orders@bookpoint.co.uk

British Library Cataloguing in Publication Data
A catalogue record for this title is available from The British Library

ISBN 0 340 72546 X

First published 2000
Impression number   10 9 8 7 6 5 4 3
Year   2005 2004 2003 2002 2001

Copyright ©2000 Ina Taylor

Typeset by Nicholls McColm.
Printed for Hodder & Stoughton Educational, a division of Hodder Headline Plc, 338 Euston Road, London NW1 3BH by Printer Trento, Italy.

Contents

1 The Time of Your Life! **4**

2 Why Celebrate a Birth? **6**

3 Birth in Christianity **8**

4 Birth in Judaism **10**

5 Birth in Islam **12**

6 Birth in Sikhism **14**

7 Birth in Hinduism **16**

8 Birth in Buddhism **18**

9 Celebrating a Birth without Religion **20**

10 When Are You Old Enough? **22**

11 Commitment to Christianity **24**

12 Commitment to Judaism **26**

13 Commitment to Sikhism **28**

14 Commitment to Hinduism **30**

15 Commitment to Buddhism **32**

16 Why Get Married? **34**

17 Marriage in Christianity **36**

18 Marriage in Judaism **38**

19 Marriage in Islam **40**

20 Marriage in Sikhism **42**

21 Marriage in Hinduism **44**

22 Marriage in Buddhism **46**

23 Design Your Own Marriage Ceremony **48**

24 Divorce 1 **50**

25 Divorce 2 **52**

26 What Does Death Mean to You? **54**

27 Christian Funerals **56**

28 Jewish Funerals **58**

29 Islamic Funerals **60**

30 Sikh Funerals **62**

31 Hindu Funerals **64**

32 Buddhist Funerals **66**

33 How Do You Celebrate a Life? **68**

34 What Next?
Islam, Judaism and Christianity **70**

35 What Next?
Hinduism, Buddhism & Sikhism **72**

36 What Next?
Reincarnation and Déjà vu **74**

37 What Next? Out-of-body
and Near-death Experiences **76**

38 What Next?
Angels, Ghosts, Spirits or Oblivion? **78**

Glossary **80**

Index **80**

The Time of Your Life!

HOW DO YOU VIEW LIFE?

It is very hard to visualise life. We are never in a position to see both ends at once, but we can look around us and see other people at different stages of theirs. The path of life is a favourite expression and one way of viewing it. It is easy to imagine a path going through all sorts of different terrain, up a steep hill, along a sandy beach, blocked by barbed wire, through mud or with an amazing view over the surrounding countryside.

Where the path actually goes to may not be obvious.

CELEBRATING THE LANDMARKS IN LIFE

There is nothing new about celebrating the stages of life, or rites of passage as they can be called. In fact it is as old as the hills. Most primitive societies had some sort of ritual to mark milestones in life like birth, puberty and death. The ceremonies are a chance for everyone to get together and celebrate life. Even funerals do that.

Today we celebrate rites of passage with just as much interest – the silver wedding, the 18th birthday party and the family funeral all get people together. It is a chance to strengthen family ties and friendships, to unite everybody. People also want to share their delight at the birth of a baby, the beginning of a loving

4

Life is 'like a river – small at first, narrowly contained within its banks, and rushing passionately past boulders and over waterfalls. Gradually the river grows wider, the banks recede, the waters flow more quietly, and – in the end – without any visible break, they become merged in the sea, and painlessly lose their individual being. The man or woman who, in old age, can see his or her life in this way, will not suffer from the fear of death, since the things they care for will continue.'

BERTRAND RUSSELL

However, when it comes to the major landmarks in life, many people turn to religion to help them express their deepest feelings. This book looks at the way the six major world religions celebrate these times of your life and also considers what other meaningful ways there might be. However, it is worth remembering that even within these religions there can be wide variations. Within the Christian Church for instance, there is a difference of opinion about ritual celebration. The Orthodox Church finds great meaning in ritual whereas a nonconformist group, called the Quakers, prefers a very simple form of worship with as little ritual as possible.

WHAT DO YOU THINK?

1 Do you think celebrating rites of passage really only matters to old people?

2 Why do you celebrate your birthday? You have had plenty before and you will have even more in the future.

5

relationship or to share their sadness at the loss of someone. Getting people together for a ceremony provides an opportunity to make a public statement. It might be to announce the name of a new person, or to declare a couple's intentions towards each other, or to say goodbye.

RITUAL AND SYMBOLISM

Because ceremonies mark major landmarks in life, many come at emotional times. It is not always easy to put emotions into words. For that reason we look for other ways. Music can be helpful in creating the mood for a lively party or for quiet reflection. Poetry readings often work better than prose in conveying a feeling and so can actions. Think how often giving flowers is a meaningful gesture – a red rose for a lover, a pot plant taken to the old lady in hospital, a bunch of flowers left by the roadside – they require no explanation. For that reason many rites of passage are accompanied by a symbolic action. This might be a lucky horseshoe given to a bride or a small amount of water poured over the head of a new baby. The action may be commonplace but it is full of meaning.

Religion plays an important part in some people's everyday life. Other people give religion little thought as they go about their daily life.

Things to do

1 In groups of four plan a board game called 'The Time of Your Life'. You need to decide what image of life will form the centre piece of the board and what landmarks the players will pass as they go round. How will you decide who has won? Is it the first person to die? Or could there be a way of gaining points during the life? You could, of course, consider reincarnation as an option!

2 Decide which image of life you think is the most helpful and draw it. Mark some of the important stages on your drawing.

3 List the things you think are an important part of celebrating a rite of passage, e.g. food or music.

4 Make a list of six events you have celebrated in the last twelve months. Why were they special?

Why Celebrate a Birth?

There are lots of babies around. The world's population is approximately six billion, that is equal to all the people who have ever lived up to this century. If the world's population is growing at such an alarming rate, why celebrate the birth of a baby? Do you think there is any point in celebrating the birth of a third baby? After all, the family has been through it all before. And what about the teenage girl who says: 'It was an accident'. Does anyone celebrate the birth of her baby? The answer is yes to both questions.

Every baby is a unique human being and new life is always precious. People feel the birth of a baby is a really special event, whatever the circumstances of conception or birth. Each individual belongs to the community of the world.

WHAT HAPPENS WHEN YOUR NEIGHBOUR HAS A BABY?

The chances are your Mum will go and visit the new mother and baby in hospital. Why does she do that? Hasn't she seen a baby before?

- List six possible presents visitors might take.
- Consider who the presents are actually for and the idea behind choosing those items. After all the baby isn't going to eat grapes and it is unlikely the new mum is starving! What about the cards that are sent? They aren't for the baby's benefit because he or she can't read. Why do people bother? What do they mean by these actions?

WHY ARE PEOPLE SO PLEASED ABOUT A NEW BABY?

- A baby is new life. There is always pleasure in new life whether it is a tiny kitten or the first snowdrop after the winter. Both seem pure and innocent and show that life goes on.
- A baby belongs to the next generation, ensuring the family won't die out.
- A family might be happy because this is the first girl (or boy) born in the family for ages.
- A baby strengthens a relationship and makes the couple into a family.
- This baby might be the first grandchild and some people are delighted to become grandparents.
- Some people might see the baby as a present from God.
- There will be happiness and relief that the baby is born healthy and that the mother is fit and well.

Would you agree with all of these points? Are there any others you want to add?

WHAT IS IN A NAME?

After all the cooing over a baby in hospital, the presents, the cards and the visitors, you might think there was no need of further ceremonies. But there is, the baby needs a name. One parent has to register the name officially at the Registry Office but that is just a matter of filling in a form – hardly an occasion for the family to get together. Many people think some public naming ceremony is needed because of the importance of your name to you. It stays with you for the rest of your life. Your first name is personal. Friends call us by our first name, strangers do not.

Names often have meanings. They can refer to special qualities like kindness, beauty or strength. Is it a nice idea to wish one of these qualities on a child? Or is it an embarrassment to be called something you obviously are not?

What do you think of the parents who give their baby the first name of every player in their favourite football team? It is probably a great laugh so long as you are not the one who has to ask for extra time and paper at the *start* of an exam, just to write your name down!

DOES IT MATTER WHEN YOU WERE BORN?

In this old rhyme, the day you were born decides your character.

> **Monday's child is fair of face**
> **Tuesday's child is full of grace**
> **Wednesday's child is full of woe**
> **Thursday's child has far to go**
> **Friday's child is loving and giving**
> **Saturday's child works hard for**
> **its living**
> **And the child that's born on**
> **the Sabbath Day**
> **Is bonny, blithe,**
> **good and gay.**

(It's worth mentioning that the word 'gay' has changed its meaning over the years and when this poem was first around, it meant 'cheerful' or 'happy'.)

Do you think the day of the week you were born on affects your personality? If not, what about the month? Magazines think enough people believe in this to feature horoscopes. Even if you don't believe in zodiac signs, it is likely you know which star sign you were born under. Could a Capricorn really be different from a Taurus? A recent insurance survey showed that people born under Pisces or Libra made more motor insurance claims than others. Coincidence?

WHAT DO YOU THINK?

1 If there is any truth in horoscopes would that mean your life is already mapped out for you? Do you have the freedom to make choices or is it already 'in the stars'?

2 The chances are you can't remember your first birthday, but it was probably celebrated. Why do you think parents bother?

3 In *Romeo and Juliet* Shakespeare wrote: *'What's in a name? That which we call a rose by any other name would smell as sweet.'* What did he mean? Would you feel a different person if everyone called you by another name from now on?

Things to do

1 Write a letter from a man to his sister. He has just been to visit his first grandchild born in hospital. What do you think he will say about his feelings when he looked at his youngest relative?

2 In groups make a poster of wishes. Decide on a shape to use. Everybody has three shapes and writes three things they would wish a new baby. The shapes can be decorated, cut out and assembled on a sheet of sugar paper.

3 Choose two people from the list below and describe how they might react to the birth of a new baby:

(i) the husband
(ii) the baby's sister
(iii) the local vicar
(iv) the mother who gives birth in a famine stricken part of Africa
(v) somebody who is an aunt for the first time
(vi) the boyfriend.

Why would some of those in the list react differently?

Birth in Christianity

CHRISTIAN PRAYERS AT BAPTISM

- *I give you this sign, for now you belong to Christ the Light of the World. Let your light shine before men that they might see your good works and give glory to your Father who is in heaven.*
- *I baptise you in the name of the Father, and of the Son and of the Holy Spirit.*
- *Receive this light: this is to show you that you have passed from darkness to light.*

Christians believe that children are a blessing from God to enable humans to take part in God's work of creation. Because of this many Christian groups consider the birth of a child to be a religious event and choose to have a religious ceremony to welcome the child into the world. Some groups, however, like Quakers and Baptists, prefer a person to choose their own religion when they are old enough to decide for themselves, so they do not baptise babies.

THE MEANING OF BAPTISM

A baby is usually welcomed into the family of the Christian Church by public baptism a few weeks or months after birth. Baptism is an opportunity to give thanks for the baby's safe delivery and to announce his or her name in public. Christians also believe that God grants the child **salvation** through baptism. This means God gives a special blessing that will save the person from sin and enable them to go to heaven at the end of their life. Because baptism also marks that person's entry into Christianity, the font was traditionally placed at the back of a church near the door. Today, where possible, the ceremony is held at the front of the church during a Sunday morning service, so that everyone feels part of what is going on and can welcome the baby into their community.

THE CEREMONY

Parents go to see the priest beforehand to talk about the baptism. This is because the priest wants to be sure they understand what they will be asked to take on when they make promises about bringing up their child as a Christian. To help them with this important task, they will need to choose godparents or sponsors. Friends are often chosen and they make the same promises as the parents at the ceremony. In a Roman Catholic ceremony it is usual to have one godfather and one godmother for the child. At an Anglican baptism there are often two godparents of the same sex as the child plus one other. The godparents agree to help with the child's spiritual and moral welfare as well as look after the child should anything happen to the parents.

On the day of the ceremony parents and sponsors arrive with the baby, who is either dressed in white or wrapped in a white shawl to symbolise

This is a traditional font made of white stone. It has a lining like a bowl, to hold the water. In some modern churches the font is on a portable wooden stand so it can be taken to the front.

purity. This part of the service takes place at the font with the parents and godparents standing by the priest.

Prayers are said asking God to receive the baby into the Christian family through baptism. The parents and godparents are asked set questions about their belief in Christianity. After the correct responses, the priest takes the baby in his arms and asks the child's name, then announces it to everyone. The sign of the cross is made with holy water on the baby's forehead. Some of the holy water is poured over the baby's head to symbolise the washing away of all sins. At a Roman Catholic baptism some aromatic oil, that has been blessed by the bishop, is rubbed gently on the baby's forehead to show the Holy Spirit is given to the child. This is called Chrismation.

After the service many families hold a small party at home where cards and presents are given to the baby.

Water plays an important part in baptism, demonstrating the washing away of sin. Although it is frequently ordinary tap water, once a blessing has been said over it, this becomes holy water.

9

WHAT DO YOU THINK?

1 Godparents for a Roman Catholic baptism must be over sixteen. Why do you think that is insisted upon? Would you agree with it?

2 Why do you think some priests refuse to baptise a baby if the parents don't go to church? Is that fair on the baby?

3 The word christening (meaning to make Christian) is often used instead of baptism. Why do people choose that word?

Things to do

1 (i) A candle may be given to the parents at a baptism. Copy out the two quotations that refer to this.

(ii) What does it say the candle symbolises?

(iii) What do these quotations say about the way a child should act in the future?

2 Design a Baptism Certificate for All Saints Church. You need to include the name of the church, and spaces for the date, the name of the child, parents, godparents and the vicar who carried out the baptism. Add two sentences explaining the significance of baptism. Decorate the certificate with appropriate baptismal symbols.

3 In groups of three or four, act out a scene in which the new parents and the grandparents are discussing whether a baby is to be christened. The grandparents are regular churchgoers and want the baby baptised. What reasons are they going to give? The parents don't go to church and don't want the baby baptised. What reasons are they going to give?

4 (i) Why are first names often called Christian names?

(ii) Why have some churches moved their fonts to the front?

(iii) Holy water usually comes out of the tap. What makes it holy?

Birth in Judaism

Children are welcomed in Judaism as a gift from God the Creator. In the **Torah** God's first command to the people he created was to have lots of children: *He created them male and female, blessed them, and said, 'Have many children.'* Jews believe this must be obeyed. Couples should have at least two children to replace themselves. Orthodox Jews take the command literally and seek to have large families.

Family life is central to Judaism because it is through children that the beliefs and traditions are passed on. Orthodox Jews believe a person is born Jewish if their mother is Jewish. No ceremony is necessary but Jews do like to mark the arrival of a new member of their faith and show that the baby belongs to the continuing heritage of Judaism.

CELEBRATING THE BIRTH OF A GIRL

On the first **Shabbat** after a little girl's birth, her father attends the **synagogue** and is invited to the reading of the Torah scrolls. Afterwards he announces his daughter's Hebrew name to everyone. Special prayers are said for the health of mother and baby.

At a Progressive synagogue, it is customary for both parents to bring their baby son or daughter to morning service on a Shabbat soon after the birth. The baby is carried to the front for a blessing from the **rabbi**.

BRIT MILAH

The birth of a son who will carry on the family name is a cause for celebration. On the eighth day after his birth the family gather for a special ceremony called Brit Milah (in English, the covenant of cutting).

In the Torah it says that God made a covenant, or agreement, with Abraham, promising to make the Jews his special people and give them a land of their own. In return Abraham was told: *From now on you must circumcise every baby boy when he is eight days old. This will show that there is a covenant between you and me.* Circumcision is a minor operation in which the foreskin of the penis is removed. The operation can be carried out anywhere, home, hospital, even at the synagogue, but it must take place on the eighth day. Only if the baby is ill is Brit Milah postponed.

The whole family gathers for the ceremony but only men remain in the room during the surgical procedure. Arrangements are made for a mohel to carry out the operation. He is not usually a doctor, but a Jewish man specially trained in religious circumcision.

ORDER OF CEREMONY:

- morning prayers are recited by the assembled men;
- a chosen person carries the baby in;
- the baby is briefly placed in Elijah's chair;
- then the baby is placed on a cushion on the sandek's lap;
- the mohel recites a blessing and performs the operation;
- the father recites a blessing after it is finished;
- the whole group say: *As he has entered into the covenant so may he enter into the Torah, into marriage and into good deeds*;
- the boy's Hebrew name is announced;
- wine is drunk by everyone present and the family have a small party.

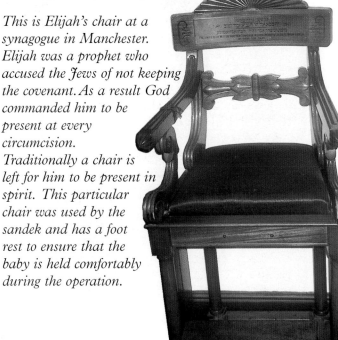

This is Elijah's chair at a synagogue in Manchester. Elijah was a prophet who accused the Jews of not keeping the covenant. As a result God commanded him to be present at every circumcision. Traditionally a chair is left for him to be present in spirit. This particular chair was used by the sandek and has a foot rest to ensure that the baby is held comfortably during the operation.

Often a relative is given the honour of being the sandek, the man who holds the baby during the circumcision.

Red wine is always an important symbol of celebration at Jewish ceremonies. Even the baby is given a few drops on his tongue after the Brit Milah before being handed back to his mother for a comforting cuddle.

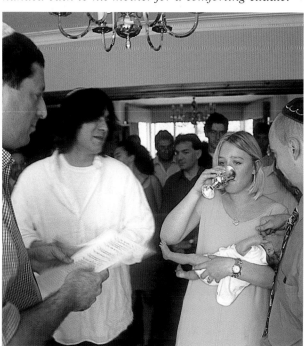

The mohel operates swiftly without anaesthetic, then puts a dressing on. The wound heals within a few days.

11

WHAT DO YOU THINK?

1 Jews say that Brit Milah looks backward to Jewish history and forward to the boy's future. In what way is this true? (Look at the blessing recited by the group of men at the ceremony.)

2 Some people might say Brit Milah is unnecessary. What do you think a Jewish family would say?

3 Jews sometimes name their baby after a relative who has died. Do you find that morbid, or a nice way of remembering someone?

Things to do

1 Design an invitation to celebrate Rebecca Levy's birth at a Progressive synagogue and to the party afterwards.

2 Find five Hebrew men's names and five women's from the Old Testament or Hebrew Bible. Can you research the meaning of any of them?

3 Write a newspaper report of David Greenbaum's Brit Milah at his home.

4 Look up and copy out the blessing which the rabbi uses to celebrate the birth in a Progressive synagogue. You can find it in Numbers 6 v24-26.

Birth in Islam

THE QUR'AN SAYS

*To Allah belongs the kingdoms
of the heaven and the earth.
He creates what He wills.
He bestows sons and daughters
according to His will.
Or He bestows both sons
and daughters,
And he leaves barren whom
He chooses
For He is full of knowledge
and power.*

12

Muslims believe every child is a gift from God and so a Muslim must marry and seek to have children. For a woman it is a great honour to become a mother. Prophet Muhammad (pbuh) explained how important a mother was in a person's life when he said: *'Paradise lies at the feet of your mother.'* So Muslims believe there are few things more important in life than having children and bringing them up correctly. Equally children have a religious duty to show kindness, respect and obedience towards their parents all their lives.

Muslims also believe that everyone is born a Muslim. It is simply that some parents choose to bring their children up in a different religion or none at all.

AT BIRTH

As soon after birth as possible a Muslim man will pick the baby up in his arms and whisper the Adhan into its right ear, and the Iqamat into the left ear. This may be done by the child's father, a male relative, or the religious leader, the Imam. The Adhan is the call to prayer in Arabic which begins 'Allahu Akbar' meaning 'God is greatest.' The Iqamat is the command to go and pray. By using these words to welcome the baby into the Ummah, the worldwide family of Islam, this ensures that 'Allah' is the first word the child hears.

At the same time, or soon after, an older, respected member of the family places something sweet like a tiny piece of sugar, honey or chewed date, on the baby's gum. This is called Taneek and symbolises the hope that the baby's life will be sweet and obedient to Allah. A blessing is then said over the child.

This means that the birth of a baby is the will of Allah. It is a blessing on the parents and a gift from God.

A SACRIFICE IS MADE

On the seventh day after the birth, family and friends meet together at home to celebrate the Aqiqah. In the days before, the family will have arranged for an animal to be sacrificed at a Halah abattoir. Traditionally one sheep or goat is sacrificed to celebrate the birth of a girl and two sacrificed for a baby boy. This is because the birth of a boy is considered a particular blessing. The meat is first cooked in a special way to make it sweet, then divided into three portions. A third is given to the poor, a third to friends and relatives, and the rest eaten at the Aqiqah.

Prophet Muhammad (pbuh) said, 'Pronounce as the first words to your children that there is no God but Allah.'

THE HEAD IS SHAVED

This takes place at the Aqiqah to symbolise the purity of the baby. Traditionally this hair is weighed and its equivalent weight given in gold or silver to the poor. Today the family often donate a sum of money to charity as their way of thanking Allah for the gift of their child. Even if the baby is bald, the family still want to give to charity. The baby's first hair is treated with great respect because it is part of a human being, and after the ceremony, the father carefully buries it in the ground.

Shaving the first hair off symbolises the removal of all impurity. A little olive oil or saffron is put on the head to soothe it afterwards.

NAMING

At the Aqiqah, the baby is given its name in public. Muslims take great care choosing a name and often ask the advice of an older relative, like the grandfather. A boy's name may be chosen from one of the 99 names of Allah. If this is the case, respect must be shown for this name and the word Abd is put in front because it means 'servant of'. So the name Abdullah would mean 'servant of Allah'. Other names are chosen from great Muslims in the past, so many boys are called Muhammad in honour of the prophet. A popular girl's name might be one of Muhammad's wives or daughters like Khadijah or Fatimah.

KHITAN

Muslim boys are circumcised, which means that the foreskin of the penis is removed. This is a simple operation usually carried out by a Muslim doctor before the baby comes home from hospital.

Muslims, like Jews, believe that God commanded the prophet Ibrahim to circumcise all the males in his household. Since then it has been the sign and practice of all the prophets of Allah. Prophet Muhammad said that all Muslim boys should be circumcised before the age of ten.

WHAT DO YOU THINK?

1 Islam teaches that babies are a gift from God. How would this affect the Muslim attitude to abortion?

2 Some people might say killing an animal was a strange way of saying thank you for a baby. What do you think a Muslim would say?

3 Muslims never speak of people 'converting' to Islam. They say they are 'reverting' to Islam. Why?

13

Things to do

1 Adhan, Taneek, Aqiqah and Khitan are the key words in this Muslim ceremony. Write a sentence explaining what each means.

2 Design an invitation to an Aqiqah. Remember the child has not been named yet and also that Muslims avoid drawing pictures of people or animals in a religious context to prevent idol worship.

3 Even at a happy family time Muslims remember people who are less fortunate. In what ways do they do this?

4 Draw five boxes in your book for each stage in a baby girl's birth ceremony. In each box write what happens and why it is done.

Birth in Sikhism

The true God has sent the child,
The long-lived child has been
born by destiny.
When he came and acquired
an abode in the womb
His mother's heart became very glad.

This hymn was composed by Guru Arjan to celebrate the birth of his son.

Sikhs believe:

- A life is a precious gift from God, a chance to know God and find union with him;
- A baby strengthens a marriage;
- A baby ensures the continuity of family life;
- You are a Sikh because you are born into a Sikh family but anyone is welcome to become a Sikh if they wish. No ceremony is needed to bring a baby into the religion.

Sometimes after a baby is born the parents are so pleased they want to share their happiness with others. So it is the new father who gives presents, like boxes of Indian sweets, to the family and friends, rather than the other way round.

CHOOSING A NAME

Sikhs believe choosing the right name for a person is extremely important because your name stays with you and will identify you for the rest of your life. As in all aspects of Sikh life the holy book, Guru Granth Sahib, plays a central part. By opening the holy book at random and taking the first letter of the word on the top of the left-hand page for the name, Sikhs believe they are allowing God to influence the choice of name. A person converting to Sikhism would chose a Sikh name this way and so would many Sikhs naming their new business.

Many names have meaning. If the letter S was given, the family might consider Sumed meaning wise or Sukhbir meaning happy or brave. Meanings are important. Sikhs believe a person should never defile their name by their actions. The same name can often be used for a girl or a boy. It is only by looking at the next name can

you tell the gender. The tenth guru gave the name Singh (meaning brave as a lion) to male Sikhs and the name Kaur (meaning princess) to female Sikhs.

It is customary for the baby naming ceremony to take place about two weeks after the birth at the end of service at the **gurdwara**. This allows the parents to take part in worship and thank God for giving them a baby, as well as to announce the name in public.

THE CEREMONY AT THE GURDWARA

1. Parents, family and friends attend the gurdwara with the baby. The parents may give a beautiful new covering for the Guru Granth Sahib, or money to the gurdwara, as a sign of their gratitude for the child. Food is also brought to be cooked and shared with everyone after the ceremony.

2. The **granthi** is the man or woman who reads from the Guru Granth Sahib. This person also prepares a sacred mixture of sugar and water called **amrit**. Prayers are recited as amrit is stirred and God's blessing is asked for the child.

I present this child and with Thy Grace
I administer to him/her the amrit.
May he/she be a true Sikh,
May he/she devote him/herself to the
service of his/her fellow men and
motherland,
May he/she be inspired with devotion,
May the holy food be acceptable
to the congregation.
By the ever-increasing glory of your name
May the whole creation be blessed.

3. The granthi drips some of the sacred amrit on the baby's lips from a ceremonial sword called the **khanda.** The rest of the amrit is given to the mother to drink.

4. The granthi opens the Guru Granth Sahib at random and reads out the first letter of the

14

first word at the top of the left-hand page. The parents can choose what the name will be. Some are able to decide there and then, others return the following week to tell everyone. When the name is announced prayers are said for the baby to grow up to be a true Sikh and show devotion to God.

5. Everyone is handed a small amount of the holy food Karah Parshad to eat. This mixture of butter, sugar and scmolina is shared at the end of every gurdwara service, symbolising the unity of the congregation.

6. Some families arrange for Akhand Path, a continuous reading of the Guru Granth Sahib from beginning to end, to celebrate the birth. This can be in the gurdwara or at home, if a copy of the holy book can be kept there with suitable respect. The baby is often given a kara, a steel bracelet worn on the right wrist, to symbolise the oneness of God. This will be exchanged for a larger size as the child grows.

A Sikh family may consult a book like this to choose a name.

WHAT DO YOU THINK?

1 Could opening a book at random allow God a chance to influence events?

2 Have you ever considered the meaning of your name? Would it affect your daily life?

3 Sikhs believe this is not the first life most of us have lived on earth. Do you?

Things to do

1 Name the two holy foods used in a Sikh naming ceremony? How are they used?

2 Look at the references to these holy foods in the quotation in the yellow box. Explain the meaning of their use in your own words.

3 Names in Sikhism tend to be uni-sex. Can you think of ten names in current use that are uni-sex? Do you like the idea of a uni-sex name?

Birth in Hinduism

THE SCRIPTURES SAY:

- *I perform this ceremony to make you attain life, power, wealth and strength.*
  I cut your hair for your long life, fame and prosperity.
- *Be a stone, be an axe, be imperishable gold.*
- *May your life be as precious as gold.*
  This will depend on your good thoughts, speech, deeds and behaviour.
- *Oh dear child, I give you this honey and ghee which has been provided by God who is the producer of all the wealth of the world.*
  May you be preserved and protected by God and live in this world for a hundred autumns.

16

A BABY IN HINDUISM

Hindus welcome a baby as a new life, but not as a new soul because they believe your soul carries the effects of good and bad deeds from a previous existence. The consequence of thoughts and actions in one life affecting the next life is called karma.

BEFORE BIRTH

Some couples go to the temple to pray for the kind of child they would like, even before its conception. Others wait until the mother is pregnant to conduct their first ceremony which can be at home or in the temple. Flowers are offered at a shrine and prayers said for a healthy pregnancy.

AFTER THE BIRTH

Most people wash a baby soon after it is born, but for Hindus this has the added significance of cleansing the baby of any impurities from its

previous life. The exact time and date of the birth is noted so the priest can work out the baby's horoscope. At birth it is traditional for the father to dip a gold item, like a ring, into honey and make the aum sign on the baby's tongue. Aum is the holy symbol of God.

Traditionally the new mother and baby stay at home and rest for the first seven to ten days. Other women in the family come in to cook and look after the household whilst the new mother

In the picture a woman offers milk to the shrine of Shiva as she prays the god will give her more children.

concentrates on looking after the baby and building up her strength. After this time the priest comes to the house to say prayers to cleanse the mother. From then on she is able to enter the kitchen and gradually resume family duties like cooking. But it is not until 40 days after the birth that she goes outside, which helps to keep her and the baby free from infection.

NAMING

The priest will have worked out the baby's horoscope based not just on the date and time of birth but also the place of birth, the parents' names and the positions of the stars and planets. Using this information he gives the parents the first letter to choose the baby's name. Hindus believe the meaning of your name can influence your personality, so careful thought is given to the name. Sometimes the priest is asked to give a name as well as a letter. A child is usually given more than one name, a public name and a private one for religious use. The name chosen might be connected with the star the baby was born under, a family deity or a quality of character.

The naming ceremony takes place in front of a holy fire which can be brought to the house in a portable container. The baby is washed and dressed in new clothes then held by the priest or father. He whispers in the baby's ear 'Your name is …' Prayers are recited for the baby to be given long life as well as virtues like strength and wisdom. It may well be an older female member of the family who is given the honour of announcing the baby's name to the family. The occasion is one for celebration with food and singing.

For most Hindu mothers the first outing with the baby is to the temple to give thanks for the safe delivery of the child. Offerings of flowers, fruit or incense are placed at the shrines of various deities in gratitude. Some orthodox Hindu families also say special prayers when the baby is around the age of six months, marking the time when he or she takes their first solid food.

MUNDAN – THE HAIR CUTTING

This usually takes place when the child is around a year old or cuts his or her first tooth. The exact timing depends on favourable star signs. It is a major occasion held at the temple with the sacred fire and a priest to perform the rituals. The child is held by a senior member of the household while the hair is cut and the head shaved. This symbolises the removal of bad karma, enabling the child to have a fresh start in life. Then something soothing and pure, like yoghurt, is smoothed onto the scalp. The hair is carefully collected because it is respected as part of a human. Some Hindus burn it in the sacred fire, others bury it in the earth near the family's ancestral home in India or else place it in the holy River Ganges to be carried away.

17

Things to do

1 Some Hindus celebrate a baby's first outing, first solid food and first hair cut. List the various 'firsts' parents like to record in their baby book?

2 Design an invitation to be sent to members of Mr & Mrs Sharma's family, inviting them to the hair cutting of their son Mahesh. Include the sacred fire in your decoration.

3 Look at the scripture quotations.
(i) List the different things that are wished for the baby.
What is prayed for most often?
(ii) Which of those quotations is used just after birth? How do you know?
(iii) When a Hindu wishes a child to be like a stone, an axe and like gold, what sort of virtues are intended?
(iv) Which quotation is recited at the mundan? What qualities are prayed for then?

WHAT DO YOU THINK?

1 Do you think a baby is born innocent or carries the sins of a previous life?

2 For many Hindus abortion is a great sin. Why would they think that?

3 *'You reap what you sow.'* What connection might that saying have with the idea of karma?

Birth in Buddhism

Buddhists have no prescribed ritual to welcome a baby into the world, nor do they feel that birth is an event of religious significance. Nevertheless many Buddhist parents want to give their child a name in public and wish it well for the future. Various naming ceremonies have grown up reflecting the culture or traditions of the country where the family lives. In Britain, where there are many different Buddhist groups, some baby naming ceremonies share common elements and involve the **sangha**, the Buddhist community of monks and lay people.

CHOOSING A NAME

Much care is given to choosing a name because Buddhists believe your name is an essential part of you. In Britain the child of Buddhist parents may have an English name but will probably also have a Buddhist name. The parents may ask the monks in the sangha to name the child, or to give them a list of possible Buddhist names they could choose. Buddhist names always have a meaning or historical significance. It could be the name of an important person from Buddhist history or may denote a positive quality like wisdom or kindness. The child is encouraged to live up to their name.

OFFERINGS

Once a date for the naming ceremony has been fixed with the sangha, family and friends are invited. On the day the parents bring flowers to lay on the shrine in front of the statue of the Buddha. They also light the candles and incense sticks to show their respect for the Buddha and his teachings. The parents sit in front of the shrine with their child and the monks sit to one side. It is traditional for the family to offer food to the monks who live in the sangha. Money is also donated towards the temple's upkeep.

THE ROLE OF THE MONKS

Monks do not have to be present at a naming ceremony. The naming could be carried out in the presence of other lay Buddhists, but Buddhist parents like the monks to be there to bless their child.

After the offerings to the shrine, the monks chant words from the scriptures. This will include the important Buddhist statement called the Three Refuges:

I take refuge in the Buddha
*I take refuge in the **Dhamma***
I take refuge in the Sangha

This is thought to give the child a good start in life. If that child continues to practise Buddhism as they grow up they will recite the Three Refuges regularly.

The monks also chant the Five Precepts which are guidelines for Buddhist behaviour and the standard of conduct all families try to live by. The senior monk in the sangha gives a short sermon about the Buddha's teachings on family life. He then tells everyone the child's name.

THREAD TYING

Some Buddhist naming ceremonies use thread as a visible symbol. A ball of sacred thread is tied by the senior monk around the Buddha statue on the shrine then taken around the outside of everyone present: monks, friends, family and baby. It may even be tied loosely around

The shrine room is made ready for the naming ceremony with offerings of flowers and candles.

everyone's wrist and returned back to the statue on the shrine. The thread colour varies. White is used to symbolise purity but red is popular as the colour of love and kindness.

The thread unites everybody in directing goodwill and love towards the baby. Sometimes a little piece of the sacred thread is broken off and remains tied loosely around the baby's wrist until it falls off in its own time.

This female monk waits for the arrival of the parents with their baby. The thread that is to be used in the ceremony is on the silver dish at her side.

WATER

In some naming ceremonies water is used symbolically. A jug of water is placed by the shrine at the start of the ceremony and the thread is passed through the handle so the jug of water is inside the circle. The senior monk sprinkles a little water from this jug on the child's head before giving a blessing. In this way, it is believed the child will be purified from any bad influences that have been carried forward from its previous existence and protected from any negative forces

in this life. Some Buddhists also shave the baby's head as another symbolic demonstration of purification.

SADHU! SADHU! SADHU!

At the end of the ceremony blessings are chanted for the child and the family. Then everyone shouts 'Sadhu!' three times. This is Pali for 'Cheers!' or 'Well done!'. In some ceremonies the group shower rose petals around the baby, as a sign of everyone's good wishes for the child's future.

WHAT DO YOU THINK?

1 Several of the rituals in a Buddhist baby-naming ceremony involve wishing the baby good for the future. Do you think this has any meaning or is it just superstition?

2 Do you think people understand the meaning of ceremonies better if there are symbolic actions to watch?

3 Would it matter to you if part of a ceremony was in a language you did not understand?

Things to do

1 Write a letter to a relative who has been invited to a Buddhist baby naming ceremony. Give them some guidance about the form the ceremony will take. Explain why you want them to be there even though they are not Buddhist.

2 Design a poster to be displayed at the Buddhist temple announcing the forthcoming naming ceremony of a baby girl who is to be called Ashoda.

3 Can you find out what the Five Precepts are? Would they be any help in bringing up a child?

4 How do Buddhists use thread in a baby naming ceremony? What is the point of it?

Celebrating a Birth without Religion

Obviously the birth of your first baby is as much an important landmark in your life as it is in the child's life. Surely this is worth celebrating. Some people think that you cannot have a 'Baby Ceremony' if you don't belong to a religion, but that's not true. There are no rules and you can design your own ceremony and make it as meaningful as you want, as well as mark the occasion with a party for friends and relatives.

Humanists are people who do not believe in a god and have no religious connections, but they do believe the birth of any new human being is important and should be marked by a special occasion. There is no set Humanist ceremony but parents are given the opportunity to say what they intend to do for their child. Friends are often asked to help them carry them out these duties. The baby is given its name and some special action is included to mark the occasion.

CHOOSING SUPPORTING ADULTS

Some parents arrange for their child to have an adult who will be a special friend to the child. That person agrees to take a special interest in the child's development and to be someone outside the family the child can turn to for help at any time. This might be necessary if the child falls out very badly with their parents, or their parents split up, or they die.

THE CEREMONY

This can be held anywhere. Home often seems appropriate with close relatives and friends invited. Some families like to make it into a special celebration by choosing favourite pieces of music and readings from poems or stories that express their hopes for the baby.

After the parents and supporting adults have said what they intend to do for the child, the baby is given a name. This is a very significant part of the ceremony because the name shows the child's individuality and uniqueness. Once you have a name you are distinct from all other human beings.

To mark the occasion some people like to toast the baby with champagne or cut a cake. Others choose to plant a tree that will grow as the child grows and possibly go on to develop flowers or fruit. At some ceremonies everyone presents the baby with a rose bud as a symbol of the beauty of the life that will open for the child. Others light a candle because the flame represents life and the warmth of human love.

A CELTIC BENEDICTION

The peace of the running water to you,

The peace of the flowing air to you,

The peace of the quiet earth to you,

The peace of the shining stars to you,

And the love and the care of us all to you.

AN AMERICAN INDIAN SONG

May the sun bring you new energies by day;

May the moon softly restore you by night.

May the rain wash away any worries you may have

And the breeze blow new strength into your being.

And then, all the days of your life,

May you walk gently through the world

And know its beauty.

WELCOMING A STEP FAMILY OR AN ADOPTED CHILD

These children will obviously have their own birthdays but they are entering a new family. Everyone hopes it will turn out well. Could you design a ceremony to celebrate this? The people involved may be teenagers; how could you give the occasion meaning without it being embarrassing?

Things to do

Design your own A4 leaflet for a birth ceremony
It should include details about:

The place
Where would you choose to hold the ceremony?

This might depend on your wishes for the child. If you hope the child will grow up to be a great footballer then you might want the ceremony at your favourite team's ground. You might decide to use this opportunity to introduce the new baby to nature, animals or the sea. If you want the child to grow up caring about green issues, then a woodland setting with the baby laid down amongst leaves and wild flowers might be appropriate. Could you hold the ceremony at Disney World or Alton Towers? Is that tasteless or could it have meaning?

Clothes and food
Are there any particular clothes you would want to dress the child in or the people who go to your ceremony? This may well depend on what you would wish for the child. Any special colours? Blue for the sky or green for nature? Do any foods have a particular meaning?

Naming
Who is actually going to say the child's name? Do you think it might be a nice idea to tell people why you chose that name? Or possibly explain its meaning if it is relevant.

Who is to attend the ceremony?
In addition to the parents is there anyone else you would like to help the child during its life? If so, what could they say at the ceremony? Do you want to use this ceremony to introduce the baby to its relatives or to your friends? How would you do this? Is there anyone you specially want to thank for the safe arrival of the baby?

A special reading or music?
What music would you play when the baby is brought in? Is there a special poem or reading you would like to use?

Parents' responsibilities
Most parents start out with all sorts of hopes for their child and many things they want to do for their new baby. Here are some:

- look after the child;
- provide love and support the child to be independent;
- respect the child as an individual;
- encourage the child to develop physically and intellectually;
- influence the child's behaviour by setting a good example;
- help the child to develop its own opinions, beliefs, and values.

What would you include?

I wish...

Three wishes are a traditional part of all fairy stories. What three things would you wish for a child of the 21st century? Do you think a large fortune will solve everything?

When Are You Old Enough?

WHAT IS THE LEGAL AGE IN BRITAIN?

Birth Can have a bank or building society account in your name; can have your own passport from birth.

5 Must go to school or receive recognised education; can drink alcohol in private.

7 Can see a U film without an adult; can draw money from a Post Office account without a parent's signature.

10 Can be tried in court and convicted of a criminal offence.

11 Usual age for secondary education.

12 Can see a 12 film.

13 Can be employed for limited hours between 7am and 7pm.

14 Can see a PG film without an adult; can drink soft drinks in a pub; can be sent to detention centre; can be finger printed.

15 Can see a 15 film.

16 Can buy cigarettes; take part in the lottery; leave school; work full-time; drink beer or wine with a meal in restaurant; choose your own doctor; legal age for sex for girls; buy fireworks; can marry with parents' consent; leave home with parents' consent; have a moped licence up to 50cc; join the Armed Forces; can be sent to a Young Offenders Institution.

17 Can have a market stall; have a driving licence for a car.

18 Can buy alcohol; marry without parents' consent; vote; watch an 18 film; give blood; make a will; can sue and be sued; can place a bet; take out a mortgage; do jury service; change name; be sent to prison.

21 Stand for parliament; get an HGV licence.

What other things could you add?

For everything there is a season,
A time for every purpose under heaven:
A time to be born, and a time to die.

Would you say there is a right age for everything? As you can see from the table, there are quite specific ages laid down in Britain for when it is legal to do certain things. You have already passed many of those landmarks but did you really feel different the next day, or even a month later?

Maybe measuring how mature you are by the calendar is not the best method. We have probably all come across people of 18, who are legally adults but behave more like eight-year-olds. At the same time you can meet someone of twelve who is incredibly sensible and mature in their outlook. Perhaps counting birthdays is not the answer. In some tribes young people who want to be recognised as adults have to undergo trials of endurance or strength. Maybe in today's society that is not appropriate. Physical maturity is not the whole answer. We probably think emotional maturity is more important. Or is it simply a matter of recognising a person has reached puberty?

With rights come responsibilities. At the outset your parents are responsible for you. It is obviously their duty to feed and clothe you but they are also responsible for teaching various things. Some of those things will be basic survival skills like feeding yourself, learning to put your clothes on, tie shoe-laces etc. Parents are also responsible for teaching their children how to behave and fit into society, to know what is right and what is wrong. At some point each child becomes an adult and takes on these responsibilities themselves. Should the new adult promise to do certain things, or does the law cover that already?

Do you need a ceremony to mark this stage? Not everyone thinks you do; Islam has no set age or ceremony. In many ways the transition from child to adult is the most important rite of passage of all, but growing up happens naturally, you can't stop it. It does not involve free choice like getting married. Perhaps a ceremony is only designed to show the public that this child is now an adult, rather than to make the person feel different.

WHAT DO YOU THINK ?

1 When do you think you are old enough to know in your own mind that you are ready to commit yourself to a religion for life?

2 Are there any ages in the table which you think need changing?

3 Are there some things that parents should teach a child and others which school should teach? Who should be responsible for teaching a child about sex?

Things to do

1 Adulthood brings more freedom and rights, but it also brings more responsibilities. List five things an adult has to do that a child does not.

2 Look at the collage and write down the legal ages involved with the items in it. Remember there may be one age for buying the object, but a different one for using it.

3 Discuss with a partner whether it might be better to have one age for everything. If so what might it be? Is it better to have no age limit at all?

23

Commitment to Christianity

Most Christians are welcomed into the church as babies, and promises are made for them at their baptism by parents and godparents. When Christians feel ready to make their own commitment, they can ask to confirm those promises themselves.

This can be at any age so long as the priest is sure the person is mature enough to understand what they are promising. In the Anglican Church it is unusual for someone to be accepted for confirmation before their teens. As the name suggests, confirmation is a *confirming,* or agreeing with, something that has already taken place – in this case the promises made at baptism. A Christian has to be baptised before they can be confirmed. Some adults who were not baptised as babies undertake both ceremonies on the same day. Others choose a Believer's Baptism, and are confirmed later.

PREPARATION

In the Roman Catholic Church preparation for confirmation begins around the age of eight, when a child takes their First Communion. They learn to prepare for this by confessing things they have said, thought and done which were wrong. At the same time they learn how the symbols of bread and wine used in the Communion service become the body and blood of Jesus. They will attend classes to increase their knowledge of the religion. By sharing in the mass, or communion service, the child is beginning the first stage of their preparation to enter the Christian faith fully through confirmation.

Anglicans wishing to be confirmed must first attend classes taken by the priest for several months. Here they study Christian beliefs, learn the important prayers and prepare for their lives as full Christians, besides getting ready for the actual Confirmation ceremony.

Confirmation is such an important step only a bishop can take this service.

CONFIRMATION CEREMONY

Confirmation is a serious personal commitment to Christianity. Candidates for confirmation join those from other churches in the area in a ceremony taken by the bishop. Candidates often wear white as they did at baptism to symbolise purity.

The bishop asks them these questions about their beliefs:
Do you turn to Christ?
Do you repent of your sins?
Do you renounce evil?
He then asks if they believe and trust in God the Father, the Son and the Holy Spirit. After this each candidate kneels in front of the bishop, who places a hand on their head saying:
Confirm, O Lord, your servant ... with your Holy Spirit.
The laying-on of hands symbolises that the person has received the Holy Spirit, who will help them lead a Christian life.

24

In a Roman Catholic service the bishop also rubs a small amount of chrism, a holy oil, on the person's forehead with the words:
Be sealed with the gift of the Holy Spirit.

A Holy Communion service is often the last part of a Confirmation service enabling the newly confirmed Christians to kneel at the altar and take their first Communion together.

Cards and gifts like Bibles or prayer books are frequently given to the newly confirmed as a memento of this important day. From then on the confirmed person tries to lead a Christian life and take Holy Communion at least three times a year, including Christmas and Easter.

BELIEVER'S BAPTISM

Some Christian prefer to follow the example set by Jesus, who was baptised as an adult by

Immersion under water represents the washing away of sin and the death of Jesus. The priest says: 'As the body is buried under water and rises again so shall the bodies of the faithful be raised by the power of Christ.'

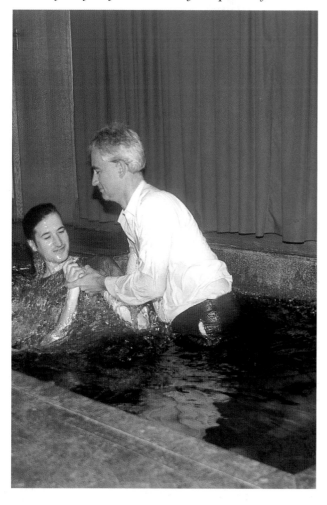

immersion in the river Jordan. There is no evidence that he baptised babies. Since it is usually too cold to hold baptisms in rivers, a small baptismal pool is sunk in the floor of some churches. People who want to become members of the church must study the faith first to be sure they understand and believe, before they undertake a Believer's Baptism.

The candidate affirms their beliefs then walks down into the pool containing water that has been blessed. The priest also stands in the pool and holds the person securely as he tips them completely under the water.

WHAT DO YOU THINK?

1 Committing yourself to a religion is a serious thing. Do you think a person of 11 or 14 years old is old enough to do this without being influenced by their friends or parents?

2 Do you think having a ritual like Believer's Baptism should be in public or are some ceremonies better held in private?

Things to do

1 Produce a leaflet to give to people enquiring about Believer's Baptism. Explain what it is and who can take part, plus a few useful tips like the water is warm and white garments can become transparent when they get wet so wear a swimming costume underneath!

2 (i) Can anyone be confirmed?
(ii) What does the word confirmation mean?
(iii) How is Believer's Baptism linked to the death and resurrection of Jesus?

3 Write a reply to this letter in a magazine: 'My mother wants me to be confirmed because she goes to church a lot. I don't know what I believe, but I do go to church sometimes. What should I do?'

Commitment to Judaism

This is the letter Eliot wrote to his aunt Sarah in Australia:

'Thirteen is the age for keeping the commandments.'
Talmud

A BOY COMES OF AGE IN JUDAISM

From ancient times thirteen has been an important age in Jewish society. From that age a boy could give evidence in court and any promise he made was legally binding. Not surprisingly Jews felt a boy was certainly old enough to understand the rights and responsibilities of leading a Jewish life. After the age of 13 a father is no longer responsible for his son's actions and the boy can keep the commandments himself.

As a sign of this new responsibility, the boy wears a prayer shawl called a **tallit** for morning prayers. The tallit has 613 strands on the fringe, each one represents a commandment he must now keep, and there is a ceremony in the synagogue to mark this important occasion.

Reaching 13 is called **Bar Mitzvah**, meaning son of the commandment. As a Bar Mitzvah boy he:
● should wear his tallit for morning prayers;
● can be called up to read the Torah at the synagogue;
● must keep the annual fast at Yom Kippur;
● can be a member of the minyan, the ten adult male Jews necessary to hold a service.

Dear Aunty Sarah

I am sorry that you were not fit enough to come to England for my Bar Mitzvah. I hope that you will feel much better now the operation is over. To cheer you up I thought I'd send you a photograph of my Bar Mitzvah and tell you what it was like.

I have been studying Hebrew with Rabbi Goldsack for nearly 18 months now, but it has only been during the past few weeks that I have been standing in the bimah to read aloud from the Torah. Dad has also helped me practise my reading.

My actual birthday was on Thursday so it was on the Shabbat following that everyone gathered for the Saturday morning service at the synagogue. I was really shaking when I saw how many people were there, I can tell you. But I did feel a bit better when the rabbi asked Dad, Grandad and Uncle Leon to stand with us in the bimah when I read. It went okay, I'm pleased to say.

Afterwards we had a little celebration of food and drinks in the synagogue hall but of course the main party was on Sunday. I think everybody came! It was a good job Mum had ordered a big cake from the kosher bakery or I think we would have run out.

I am sending a photograph so you can see what the big day was like. But most of all thank you for the lovely prayer book you sent me, I will really treasure that.

Your loving nephew,
Eliot

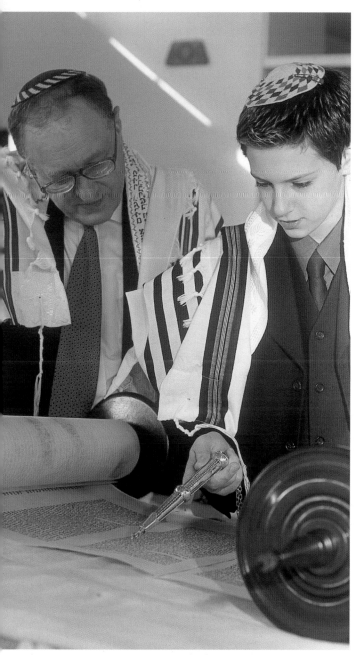

Dad took this picture at the rehearsal for my Bar Mitzvah ceremony. The rabbi is standing next to me. Can you see the silver yad I am using to point with? It was a present from granny for my Bar Mitzvah.

A GIRL COMES OF AGE IN JUDAISM

Jews believe girls mature earlier than boys and can take responsibility for their actions from the age of twelve. In the past there was no special ceremony for them but in 1922 Reform Jews introduced a ceremony called **Bat Mitzvah** (daughter of the commandment). Because Reform Jews allow women to take an equal part in synagogue worship, their Bat Mitzvah is just like the boy's ceremony.

In Orthodox Judaism women do not take an active part in synagogue worship, so the ceremony for a girl is different. It is usually held on a Sunday near her twelfth birthday in the community hall. The event may well be shared with several other girls of similar age. Each girl chooses a passage of poetry or the psalms to read out. She will probably give a short talk about the life of a famous Jewish woman she has studied.

The ceremony is called **Bat Chayil** which means daughter of worth. Although the girl does not have the same commandments to keep as a boy, she does have to know how to keep a Jewish home. As part of her preparation for Bat Chayil she will have learned about ceremonies connected with opening Shabbat, celebrating festivals at home, keeping kosher as well as the importance of Jewish marriage. Families usually have a small party to celebrate their daughter's coming of age.

WHAT DO YOU THINK?

1 Would you feel any different after a public ceremony marking your coming of age?

2 'Women and men are different – that's a fact of life.' Should there be different coming of age ceremonies then?

3 At a Bar Mitzvah the father says: 'Blessed is the One who has freed me from responsibility for the boy's sins.'

Why does he say this?

Things to do

1 A girl has to learn how to 'keep kosher.' Can you find out what that means?

2 Divide your page into six boxes and draw a sequence of pictures to show the preparations and the activities on the Bar Mitzvah day. Use Eliot's letter to help you.

Commitment to Sikhism

When Sikhs want to make a full commitment to their religion they ask to become a member of the Khalsa, this means literally the group of pure ones. The ceremony is also called baptism or taking amrit. It has nothing to do with a person reaching a particular age, but shows the person intends to live strictly by the rules of the Sikh religion.

Any Sikh, male or female, can ask for baptism at any age but few feel mature enough to take on such serious religious duties before they are 16.

This ceremony requires no study but candidates have to think deeply about the promises they are going to make, to be sure they intend to keep them.

THE CEREMONY

Only members of the Khalsa, that is other baptised Sikhs, are present at the ceremony. They are called the Panj Piare.

At the outset the rules of the Khalsa are explained to the candidates. Prayers are offered for God's blessing and during the ceremony at the gurdwara there are readings from Guru Granth Sahib the holy scriptures. A large metal bowl containing amrit, the sacred sugar water, is stirred by everyone in turn using the khanda, or ceremonial sword. Each candidate for baptism kneels in front of the Panj Piare and is given amrit five times in their cupped hands. This shows that in future they will never eat or drink anything that has been gained dishonestly. Five times the amrit is sprinkled on their eyes so that they do not look at evil things and five times it is sprinkled on their head to show they will grow in the faith. When all the candidates have received this, they drink the remaining amrit from the same bowl to show their unity. After final prayers everyone shares the holy food, Karah Parshad.

When Sikhs take amrit, they dress the same as Sikhs did at the time of Guru Gobind Singh.

28

THE KHALSA RULES

1. **To get up early, bath and say the morning prayers.**
2. **To say the evening prayers before going to bed.**
3. **To sing the Ardas prayer regularly.**
4. **Not to take alcohol or tobacco.**
5. **Not to have sex outside of marriage.**
6. **To give 10% of your earnings to charity.**
7. **Not to eat meat that has been ritually slaughtered.**
8. **To wear the five Ks.**
9. **To add the name Singh if you are a man and Kaur if you are a woman.**
10. **To work hard and honestly to provide for your family whilst treating other Sikhs as brothers and sisters.**

THE FIVE KS

They are called this because each object starts with the letter K. These symbols were the ones that Guru Gobind Singh told members of the first Khalsa to wear and are worn today by Sikhs of both sexes.

Kara is a steel bangle usually worn on the right wrist. It fits loosely and falls forward on to the hand reminding a Sikh of the high standard of behaviour expected of them. The circular bangle is also a symbol of one God with no beginning and no end.

Kirpan is a short dagger which is always kept in its sheath. This is a symbol of power and the freedom of the spirit, reminding Sikhs that they should fight for what is right. It must only be drawn when the religion is threatened. Many Sikhs actually carry a miniature kirpan in their pocket when they go about their everyday life and wear the ceremonial one only at the gurdwara or home.

Kachha are cotton shorts worn as underwear. They are worn as sign of modesty and, because they are easier to move around in than long robes, a symbol that a Sikh is prepared and active in all situations.

Kesh is long hair. Sikhs believe their hair is a gift from God. By keeping it clean and not cutting it, they are showing their acceptance of God's will. In men kesh is a sign of strength, and in women a sign of beauty.

Kangha is a small comb that tucks in the hair showing that their life should be clean and orderly.

AFTER THE CEREMONY

After the ceremony the new members of the Khalsa continue with normal life but take great care to live by the Sikh principles.

They also take a new name which is added on as a surname or a middle name. Men take the name Singh, meaning lion, and the women members of the Khalsa add the name Kaur meaning princess.

WHAT DO YOU THINK?

1 Do you think it makes a person's faith stronger if there are certain symbolic items they can wear?

2 Sikhs choose when to be baptised. Would it be better if there was a set age for this ceremony?

3 Look at the rules of the Khalsa. Are there any you would change or add if you were setting the standard for a good life?

Things to do

1 Look up what happened at the original ceremony Guru Gobind Singh held in 1699.

2 Make a poster to explain the symbolism of each of the five Ks.

3 (i) What does the word Khalsa mean?
(ii) Why do you think it is called that?
(iii) What other Sikh ceremonies use amrit?

4 The number five occurs many times in this ceremony. Make a list of the different occasions something to do with five is involved.

Commitment to Hinduism

In the West this ceremony is only celebrated by the most devout Hindus whose sons come from the top three varnas or castes and are likely to become priests. There is no equivalent ceremony for girls. Some Hindus might say marriage marks a girl's passage to adulthood.

THE UPANAYANA CEREMONY

Hindus believe there are four stages in a male's spiritual development. The first of these is the student stage when he leaves his father to go and learn about his religion from a guru, or spiritual teacher. This stage is marked by the Upanayana ceremony. The age at which this happens varies with the community but it is commonly between seven and thirteen. Odd numbers are always believed to be more auspicious than even numbers in Hinduism.

THE CEREMONY

As in all important events in a Hindu's life, the birth horoscope is consulted to discover the most favourable time for the ceremony. The ceremony can take place at home but more usually it is held at the Hindu temple where the holy fire can be easily kindled.

Preparations for the ceremony are symbolic.
- The boy bathes to purify his body and show he is beginning a fresh stage;
- His head can be shaved as a sign that he is accepting discipline;
- Clean or new clothes are put on for the ceremony to symbolise the new life he is entering;
- Some boys do not eat any cooked food until after the ceremony as a sign of purification.

'Oh, my child, this sacred thread is purified and will lead you to a knowledge of the Absolute. The natural source of the sacred thread is God himself and it is bestowed again and again for eternity. It gives you long life and favours thoughts of God. This thread I put round you…May it enlighten your mind.'– The father.

'My pupil, I accept you as one of my children. From now on your happiness and sorrow will be my happiness and sorrow. I place you in the hands of Almighty God. By his blessing may you enjoy a hundred autumns happily and merrily.' – The teacher.

'Let him have nothing to do with meat, perfumes, garlands, anger, jealousy, singing, dancing or playing musical instruments. He may not gamble, lie, quarrel, hurt any living creature or associate with women. The promise that he will study the holy books under a teacher must be kept until he has learned them perfectly.' – The teacher.

The father and son may go to the temple where the priest is waiting, or the ceremony may take place at home. The holy fire is lit to show the presence of God and aromatic offerings like sandalwood and incense are put on it. The boy and father sit on the ground facing the priest, who will become the boy's spiritual teacher, or guru.

The ceremony begins with the priest chanting **mantras**. As the father hands his son over to the guru, the boy promises to be a good student, obey his teacher and be self-disciplined: 'I declare before you that I will observe the vows and disciplines.'

The guru places a sacred thread diagonally across the boy's left shoulder to his right hip as a sign that he accepts the boy. From now on the boy will wear the sacred thread for the rest of his life except when he is in mourning. He only takes it off to replace it with a new one once a year.

The father feeds the holy fire ready for his son's Upanayana ceremony.

As a mark of respect to his teacher, the boy places a garland of flowers over the guru's head before reciting a prayer. The priest ends the ceremony by giving the boy some advice about his daily worship.

After the ceremony family and friends celebrate this important step in the boy's religious development with a shared meal. In the past a boy left home to go and study with his guru, but this is now rare.

In the future the boy will live according to the promises he made, pray three times a day and learn about the scriptures with the priest until he is ready to move on to being a householder, the second stage in his spiritual development.

31

WHAT DO YOU THINK?

1 Does it help to have a visible reminder of a promise, like a wedding ring? Or should a religious arrangement remain private between God and the person?

2 Find the quotation where the teacher sets out the rules the student will obey until his marriage. Are these reasonable terms for a young man?

Things to do

1 List four symbolic actions or objects in the Upanayana Ceremony and explain what they mean.

2 Write a letter from a Hindu boy in India to his cousin in England telling him about the sacred thread ceremony he has recently celebrated.

3 Research what the four Ashramas, the stages of spiritual development, are in Hinduism. The Upanayana ceremony is the first.

4 Make a poster of this ceremony. Make sure everything in it is clearly labelled and fully explained.

Commitment to Buddhism

CHOOSING TO BE A BUDDHIST

There is no ceremony that marks a person's coming of age in Buddhism. Nor is there a set way to become a Buddhist. In a Buddhist country a child born into a Buddhist family would grow up practising that way of life and not feel the need to be enrolled into the religion.

In the West many people who are Buddhists have chosen to make that commitment at some point in their adult life. Then they can approach the sangha, the Buddhist community of monks and lay people, and ask if they can 'Take the Refuges' (see page 18). The sangha probably knows them already and is aware they have considered the matter deeply. Provided the request was made for the right reasons, they would agree. There are no classes that they have to attend.

Most Buddhist groups don't usually look for converts, they believe the request will come when someone feels ready. In practice few sanghas would feel a person under 16 was ready to make a commitment to Buddhism, more likely they would be over the age of 20. If someone younger asked, they might be advised to follow the Five Precepts a little longer before taking the Refuges. The Five Precepts are guidelines, not rules, for living a Buddhist life.

THE CEREMONY

The ceremony can be very quiet and private with the person sitting in front of a Buddhist teacher, or any lay Buddhist. It is the motivation that matters more than the ritual. Some sanghas hold large public ceremonies in the shrine room if a whole family requests to become Buddhist together.

The type of clothing is not important. Many people choose to wear white to represent the cleanliness of their heart and mind. The person will make an offering at the shrine, usually putting flowers down and lighting an incense stick. A monk may give a short talk addressed to the new Buddhists giving guidance on following the Buddhist way of life. Then each person who wants to make the commitment will recite the Three Refuges and Five Precepts.

From then on as lay members of the sangha, these Buddhists will support the monks and in return receive teachings from them to assist in their search for enlightenment.

> ### THE FIVE PRECEPTS
> 1. **To refrain from harming any living thing.**
> 2. **To refrain from taking what is not freely given.**
> 3. **To refrain from adultery.**
> 4. **To refrain from wrong speech.**
> 5. **To refrain from taking intoxicating drinks and drugs that cloud the mind.**

A DEEPER COMMITMENT

A few Buddhists choose to take their commitment a stage further and become a monk or nun for a period of time. The time can vary from a week, a few months, several years or even for the rest of their life. They choose this way of life in order to practise self-discipline and to devote some of their time to following the Buddhist path to enlightenment.

TRYING OUT THE MONASTIC LIFE

In some eastern Buddhist countries it is traditional for boys to enter the monastery for a few years as novice monks (that is learner monks) from the age of eight. Whilst these children are expected to try and live according to the Ten Precepts like adult monks, the monastery is actually providing the boys with a secondary education they would not otherwise receive. Most leave in their teens to resume their normal life.

Some young Buddhists enter a monastery as

novices during the school holidays. Their stay is short and it develops their knowledge of Buddhism. It is a sign that they are ready to take responsibility for themselves. In Thailand and Burma, it is seen as 'a coming of age' event.

BECOMING A MONK OR A NUN

Only a person over the age of 20 is considered mature enough to ask to become a full Buddhist monk. Even this can be for a short period, like three months. In some Buddhist traditions women can become monks, joining a group of other women (see photograph on p19).

THE CEREMONY

A person who wants to become a full monk must have their parents' permission, or if they are married, the permission of their wife. Senior monks from the community will talk to the candidate to ensure his suitability, namely that he is a free man, owes no money and is healthy. If that is so and the person has his robes and alms bowl, he can approach the sangha for permission

This man has just made his commitment to Buddhism in front of the shrine. He is being greeted by members of the lay community and given presents.

to enter. Once the whole sangha has agreed, he is ordained as a monk and may be given a new name to inspire him in his future life.

THE TEN PRECEPTS

A monk interprets the third precept to mean he must lead a celibate life, that is one without sex. In addition he adds these extra Five Precepts to the ones on the previous page:

> 6. **To refrain from eating after noon.**
> 7. **To refrain from dancing, singing and unseemly entertainment.**
> 8. **To refrain from the use of perfumes, garlands and things to beautify the person.**
> 9. **To refrain from sleeping on a luxurious bed.**
> 10. **To refrain from handling money.**

33

WHAT DO YOU THINK?

1 Some people would say there is no point in being a monk just for a few weeks. How would a Buddhist answer that?

2 What does a Buddhist mean by 'taking refuge'? Look back to page 18 for help.

3 Buddhists are concerned not to cause suffering. Why do you think they insist a person gets permission from their parents or spouse before becoming a monk?

Things to do

1 What can you discover about the life of a Buddhist monk?

2 Express the first Five Precepts in your own words to make them easier to understand.

3 Draw a logo for a new Buddhist sangha that is based on the Three Refuges, which are also called the Three Jewels.

Why get Married?

WHAT IS MARRIAGE?

Sometimes a couple decide that they have such love and respect for each other that they want to tell everyone. So they choose to declare their love for each other and their hopes for their future life together in the presence of friends and family.

People's views about what marriage means vary tremendously. Probably one thing everyone is agreed on: marriage is more than love and sex. Many people experience love and sex outside of marriage, so there has to be something extra that comes with marriage.

- One important feature is that marriage is intended to be a long-term relationship. At the time they get married, a couple hope and expect that their relationship will last for the rest of their lives. Sadly this is not always the case.

- An important characteristic of marriage is that it involves mutual love and respect. If one of the couple did not actually love or care about the person they were marrying, most of us would ask, 'Why are you getting married then?' In a marriage each partner is responsible for looking after the other one. 'In sickness and in health' is a favourite saying. It also means that they will look after their partner through the really bad times as well as the good times.

- Many people believe that both partners are responsible for whether the marriage works or fails.

- Children are an important part of marriage. If there are children, both partners in the marriage share responsibility for bringing them up.

IS MARRIAGE FOR EVERYBODY?

Certainly no one has to marry, but marriage is very popular. Statistically most people will get married at least once in their lifetime. Some will get married more than once which suggests that even when it has gone wrong, they still feel marriage is a special relationship worth trying again. Some people delay marrying until they are older and want to have children.

Some people agree with all those points above about marriage but if their relationship is with a person of the same sex, they are denied a legal or a religious marriage. They can, however, arrange to celebrate their gay relationship with their family and friends and go on to live together in a loving relationship.

Marriage is not for everyone. Some people prefer to live on their own and others do not find the partner they want. They are not weird. They simply find life more fulfilling by themselves, when they can choose to socialise with whoever they like, for as long as they like, but still retain their independence. Their relationships with other people may contain love and sex but there is no long-term commitment.

Some people find greater fulfilment in celibacy. This is a life with no sex, or one in which sex is given up for a time. Those choosing a celibate life find that it helps them to concentrate all their energies on what is most important to them at that time.

HOW DO PEOPLE CHOOSE SUITABLE PARTNERS?

There are lots of answers to this question but no guaranteed winner! If you ask people, it often transpires that their marriage was based on a chance meeting which developed into a deeper

Is this your idea of marriage?

relationship. But is this is the best way to decide who you will spend the rest of your life with?

ARRANGED MARRIAGE

In the west you marry the person you love.
In the east you love the person you marry.

In Western cultures people would say that love was the main reason for getting married. In eastern cultures, especially those originating in the Indian sub-continent, marriages are traditionally arranged by the parents. Love develops between the couple after they are married. Statistically these marriages have a higher success rate than western love matches and that is not because divorce is forbidden.

SUPPORTERS OF ARRANGED MARRIAGE SAY:

- Parents with experience of marriage have a better idea of the sort of qualities needed in this relationship than young unmarried people.
- A person in love can be so bowled over by the other person that they ignore their faults.
- A marriage joins families, so the families should be involved in this important decision.
- The person who knows you best is probably a parent. They have lived with your good and bad points, so they will know who is likely to suit you.
- Love will grow between a couple if they are well matched.

THE DATING AGENCY

Although marriages arranged by parents are unusual in Western society now, dating agencies are popular. Is this a more reliable way of finding the right marriage partner than leaving it to chance?

SUCCESSFUL professional male, 45, enjoys sports, horse riding, would like to meet assertive female. any age for friendship & fun. Staffs. 1455 (phone only).
VERY attractive, blonde female, 32, slim, likes cinema. theatre, a social, I drink, eating out, would like to meet female, similar age for friendship etc. Cheshire 1450 (phone only).
VERY attractive female, 27, enjoys pubs, clubs, going to the gym, would like to meet male with G.S.O.H, for fun nights out etc. Cheshire. 1420 (phone only).
VERY attractive female, 29, blonde pale green eyes, slim, likes music, cinema & a social drink, looking for male for fun & friendship, etc. Lancs. 1442 (phone only)

WHAT DO YOU THINK?

1 'Love is blind.' What does it mean and could it be true?

2 How essential do you think children are to a marriage? Should you marry if you plan to have children? If you don't want, or can't have children, does that mean you shouldn't get married?

3 Living together before marrying has become a common method of testing a relationship in the West. In Eastern cultures it is usual for parents to investigate the background of their child's potential bride or groom. Which do you think is likely to succeed in the long term?

Things to do

1 Design a questionnaire for the PERFECT MATCH dating agency that can be posted out to people who have paid it to find them a suitable husband or wife. You probably need at least 20 questions and multiple choice answers that can be read by a computer. Will you have the same questions for men and women? Consider what a person would expect from a marriage rather than just a casual relationship.

2 (i) What does celibacy mean?
(ii) What sort of person might choose to be celibate for a time?

3 What is an arranged marriage? Draw up a table with two columns and list the advantages and disadvantages of arranged marriages.

4 Read the advert. What sort of impression do you get of the people who are advertising? Who do you think would be the ideal partner for the first one?

35

Marriage in Christianity

WHAT IS HOLY MATRIMONY?

Christians believe marriage is more than an arrangement between two people to live together in a sexual relationship. They regard it as a sacred relationship which has God's blessing and reflects God's love for his people. For that reason it is called 'holy'. Matrimony is simply an old-fashioned word for marriage. The Roman Catholic marriage service says: *'The love of man and woman is made holy in the sacrament of marriage, and becomes the mirror of your everlasting love.'* Because the couple make their promises to each other before God, Christians believe those promises are for life.

THE PURPOSES OF CHRISTIAN MARRIAGE

The Christian ceremony gives three clear reasons for marriage:

- That this is a relationship where a couple can look after each other throughout their life: that they *'may comfort and help each other, living faithfully together in need and in plenty, in sorrow and in joy.'*
- That marriage is the right place for a sexual relationship between a man and woman: so *'with delight and tenderness they may know each other and through the joy of their bodily union may strengthen the union of their hearts and lives.'*
- To have children and *'be blessed in caring for them, and bringing them up in accordance with God's will, to his praise and glory.'*

PREPARATION

Christians are free to marry who they like, although some groups, like Roman Catholics, encourage their members to marry others of that group. A Christian couple who want to marry would go and talk to their priest first. Besides agreeing the date, the priest will discuss the meaning of Christian marriage to make sure the couple understand exactly what they are entering into.

Banns are read out in church on three Sundays before the wedding. These are public announcements of the couple's intentions and give the opportunity for the marriage to be stopped if it is illegal. Although this is extremely uncommon, the reason might be that one of them is already married, or that the couple are too closely related, like uncle and niece.

A Christian couple marry at the altar.

The wedding ring is first placed on the prayer book.

36

The Ceremony

- The bride stands on the left-hand side of the groom facing the altar and in front of the priest who is going to take the service.
- The priest tells everyone present that they are here with God to witness the marriage of this couple. He explains the purpose of Christian marriage and asks if there are any reasons why the marriage cannot go ahead.
- The priest asks first the groom and then the bride if they wish to marry each other. If they are in agreement, the groom takes the right hand of the bride and makes his promises to her. She then takes the groom's right hand and makes her promises to him. They promise to love, comfort, honour and protect each other in sickness and in health so long as they live
- A wedding ring is first placed on the priest's open prayer book. The groom puts this ring on the third finger of the bride's left hand and makes his declaration of marriage. The bride can give a ring and make the same declaration, but she does not have to.
- The priest says a blessing over the couple.
- He joins their right hands and wraps the stole from his robes over their hands saying: *'That which God has joined together, let no man divide.'*
- The priest gives a short talk to everyone. Much of it is advice to the newly weds, as well as encouragement to everyone else to support the couple in their new life together. Hymns and prayers usually end the religious service.
- To fulfil the legal part of the ceremony, the couple sign the marriage register in front of witnesses.

WHAT DO YOU THINK?

1 How important do you think the promises made at a Christian marriage are? Does a belief in the presence of God strengthen them?

Things to do

Love is patient and kind: it is not jealous or conceited or proud; love is not ill-mannered or selfish or irritable; love does not keep a record of wrongs; love is not happy with evil, but is happy with the truth. Love never gives up; and its faith, hope and patience never fail. Love is eternal.
1 Corinthians 13 v4-8

1 This is a favourite Bible reading at Christian marriages. Go through the passage and list the various attributes love is supposed to have. If a couple could behave like this towards each other do you think it would create a successful marriage? Is it realistic, helpful or terrifying? What sort of advice would you offer for a successful marriage?

2 Make a leaflet that St Benedict's Church could give to couples who enquire about getting married there. It will need to explain why getting married there has a different meaning from getting married in a Registry Office. You should also include a brief description of the ceremony as well as helpful information about who to contact for the choir, bells and organ.

3 (i) What are banns and why are they read out?
(ii) What is the Christian attitude to having children?
(iii) Look again at the ceremony. What role do Christians believe God plays in the wedding ceremony?

4 Work out role play telephone call between the vicar and a girl who wants to get married at St Benedict's because she likes old churches but doesn't believe in God.

Marriage in Judaism

WHAT DO THE SCRIPTURES SAY?

- *'Your wife has been given to you in order that you may realise with her life's great plan.'*
  TALMUD
- *'A man without a wife is incomplete.'*
  TALMUD
- *'Find a wife and you find a good thing, it shows that the Lord is good to you.'*
  PROVERBS 18 v22

JEWISH ATTITUDE TOWARDS MARRIAGE

Jews believe everyone should marry:
- Within marriage the personality can develop and fulfil itself;
- It is the best environment for bringing up children;
- Home is where customs and traditions are passed on;
- Marriage is part of God's great plan and enables humans to take part in creation.

HOW DO YOU FIND THE RIGHT MATCH?

Because Jewish marriage is concerned with having children to carry on the traditions, there is great pressure on a young Jew to marry another Jew. It is thought there will be numerous problems if someone 'marries out' of the religion. Will their partner understand the kosher dietary rules? Will a baby son be circumcised? Another very important concern is whether the children of that marriage will be Jewish at all because Orthodox Jews believe a person is only born Jewish if they have a Jewish mother. Progressive Jews accept a person as Jewish if either or both of their parents are Jews.

Although arranged marriages are extremely rare in Judaism, matchmaking does exist. There are special Jewish 'dating agencies', as well as unofficial matchmakers, in the community to help couples meet.

CEREMONY

The basic requirements for a Jewish marriage are simple – a bride, groom, rabbi, two witnesses and a **chuppah** or marriage canopy. The marriage can actually take place anywhere. In practice families like to celebrate this union of a man and a woman in much greater style. Customs vary from country to country as Jews adapt their own traditions to those of their own country. In Britain many marriages do take place in the synagogue, but it is not unknown for a couple to marry in the garden in the summer. It says in the scriptures that the couple's children would then be as numerous as the stars in the sky – though whether a young couple would want such a large family is doubtful!

No weddings take place on Shabbat or festival days. Sunday afternoons and Tuesdays are the most popular days.

ORDER OF CEREMONY

- Couple meet under the chuppah.
- The chuppah symbolises the couple's new home. It is a covering over their head but open at the sides to welcome family and friends in.
- Red wine is a sign of celebration at many ceremonies. The groom will later sip the wine and share it with his bride as in the picture.
- Rabbi blesses the wine which the couple will drink.
- The groom gives the bride a ring as a token of their marriage. The ring is traditionally put on the index finger of her right hand first, she later transfers it to the third finger of her left hand.
- Ketubah is read.
- The ketubah is the marriage contract which is given to the wife. It is her security because her husband sets down in writing his agreement to look after her.
- The chazzan chants the seven blessings on the couple.
- It is traditional for the groom to stamp on a wine glass. This symbolises that all marriages have their good and bad times, and it also reminds Jews that although weddings are a time of joy, there is still sadness at the loss of their temple in Jerusalem in 70CE.
- Couple sign the civil marriage register.

WHAT DO YOU THINK?

1 Do you think it is helpful for a woman to have a contract setting out the terms of her marriage? Should a man have one too?

2 Do you think a matchmaker is any different from a dating agency?

Things to do

1 Make a poster to show the various stages of a Jewish wedding.

2 What can you discover about the temple that was destroyed in 70 CE? Who built it and who demolished it? Does any of it survive today?

3 Write a letter to your Jewish son who is at university, explaining why he ought to be going out with a Jewish girl.

The bride is being given a sip of wine by the groom. The chazzan, who leads the chanting, wears the large black hat. The rabbi stands on the left facing the couple. This ceremony takes place in the synagogue in front of the ark containing the holy scriptures.

Marriage in Islam

THE QUR'AN SAYS:

- *Take in marriage those among you who are single.*

- *By another sign He gave you spouses from among yourselves, that you may live in peace with them, and planted love and kindness in your hearts.*

- *It was He who created you from a single being.*
  From that being He created his mate, so that he might find comfort in her.

- *You may marry other women who seem good to you: two, three or four of them.*
  But if you fear that you cannot maintain equality among them, marry only one.

40

Friends prepare the bride for the walimah.

ISLAMIC VIEW OF MARRIAGE

For a Muslim, marriage is the cornerstone of family life. It is seen as the natural bringing together of a man and a woman to have children. Muslims believe Allah expects all Muslims to marry and have children.

Islam believes marriage is a partnership between men and women where both have rights and responsibilities. Their rights and responsibilities are equal but different. The man's duty is to provide for his wife and children, and the woman's duty is to care for her husband and children.

ARRANGED, OR ASSISTED, MARRIAGE

Muslims believe that marriage is for life and therefore should be very carefully planned. Some think romance sweeps people off their feet and leads them to make a decision they may regret later.

When a young Muslim reaches an age at which their parents think they are ready to start

their own family, the search begins for a suitable partner. If a likely partner is found, a meeting is arranged between the young people in the presence of both families. This will be the first of several meetings. If the young couple are interested in each other, they are allowed as much time as they want to decide whether they wish to marry.

Islam is very clear that both the girl and the boy have complete freedom to say no to the marriage. The Qur'an says a forced marriage is not a true marriage.

THE MAHR

One of the first things that must be decided is the mahr, or dowry. This is a sum of money which the groom pays to his intended wife to show that he respects her as a person in her own right. It also demonstrates that he can afford to keep a wife and children. The mahr is usually paid in two parts. The first part can be a sum of money paid directly to the woman, although nowadays this money often goes towards paying for the wedding or may be given to the wife in the form of jewellery. The other part of the mahr is a fixed sum of money specified in the nikah, or marriage contract. It is not usually paid over to the wife unless the husband wants a divorce.

Muhammad (pbuh) said that a bride's family should not demand a huge sum of money as the mahr, nor should they accept nothing. The mahr is important because it safeguards a woman's future should the marriage end in divorce.

Some of the mahr is paid in jewellery.

THE NIKAH

This is a contract between the two who are marrying. It is read and signed by each of them in the presence of two witnesses and before Allah. The nikah is essentially a business agreement because it sets out the amount of the mahr and any conditions a wife requests, such as that the husband will not have more than one wife.

Signing the Nikah can take place at home, in the mosque, or anywhere provided it is correctly witnessed. When the Nikah is handed over the girl is not usually present. She is represented by her father who will read the Nikah and say, *'I marry you my daughter according to Allah's Book, the Qur'an and the Sunnah of the Messenger of Allah (pbuh) and with the dowry agreed upon.'* The groom accepts using similar words.

The couple are now married under Islamic law even though the girl was not present. Civil registration of the marriage is also necessary by law. This can be at the Registry Office if the mosque is not licensed for marriage. Although married the couple do not, however, live together until after the walimah, the family reception, which may be a few weeks later.

POLYGAMY

Islam allows a man to have up to four wives at the same time provided he treats them equally. But a Muslim has to abide by the laws of the country he is living in, so in Britain for instance, only marriage to one wife is recognised legally. Women are never permitted more than one husband because the children would not know who their father was.

WHAT DO YOU THINK?

1 Can you think of any reasons why a wife might be grateful that her husband can have more than one wife?

2 Do you think receiving a mahr could be an advantage for a wife?

3 Do you think a girl is given the same freedom as a boy when it comes to marriage?

Things to do

1 Write a short newspaper article (no more than 200 words) under the headline 'Mum and Dad Know Best' explaining why Muslims prefer their parents to find a partner for them.

2 Research some information about Prophet Muhammad's (pbuh) wife Khadijah.

3 (i) Why can't a Muslim woman have more than one husband?

(ii) What is a Nikah?

(iii) In what ways do a Muslim husband and wife's duties vary?

4 Look at the quotations from the Qur'an. What reason is given for marrying only one woman at a time?

Marriage in Sikhism

THE SIKH VIEW OF MARRIAGE

Sikhs believe that marriage is a vital part of a Sikh's religious development, so all Sikhs should marry someone of the same religion. They regard marriage as a spiritual journey which will bring them nearer to God. It is believed that as the couple help each other to draw nearer to God, they will also grow closer to one another.

> **Guru Granth Sahib says:**
> - **When husband and wife sit side by side why should we treat them as two? Outwardly separate, their bodies distinct, yet inwardly joined as one.**
> - **Happy the girl, now awakened to love, when the matchmaker comes with his news.**
> - **They are not man and wife who only have physical contact, only they are wedded truly who have one spirit in two bodies.**
> - **Praise and blame I both forsake, I seize the edge of your garment, All else I let pass. All relationships I have found false; I cling to thee, my Lord.**

THE PREPARATION

Because Sikhism began in India it continued the Indian tradition of arranged marriage. For Sikhs marriage is as much the joining of two families, as it is the joining of two people. Since a girl traditionally goes to live with her husband's family, it is important for everybody's future happiness to ensure that she will fit in with them.

Changes to the arranged marriage system are coming about amongst Sikhs living in the West because couples often meet at college or work. Nevertheless both parents' permission is sought and enquiries are made about the partner's suitability before the marriage goes ahead.

Once a couple have agreed to marry, there is usually a meeting at the girl's home to give both families a chance to get to know one another better. Presents are often exchanged as a sign of their new closeness.

In the days before the wedding, the bride is helped with her preparations by her sisters and female cousins. Red is traditionally a good colour for a bride to wear at her wedding, though other colours are chosen. White, the colour of mourning, is not worn.

WHAT DO YOU THINK?

1 There is no such thing as a Sikh marriage certificate because it is thought if the ceremony is witnessed by people, a piece of paper is unnecessary. Do you see any problem with this arrangement?

2 Sikhs believe love grows as the marriage matures, so it is unnecessary for a young couple to be in love before the wedding. What do you think?

3 The couple make no promises at a Sikh wedding. Do you think it better not to ask people to make promises they do not know if they can keep?

Things to do

1 What do you think a Sikh family would say if their daughter asked permission to marry a Christian? Why?

2 A Sikh would say that Guru Granth Sahib is central to their life and their religion. How is it central to the marriage ceremony?

3 Write a newspaper report about a Sikh wedding for the 'Coventry Herald'. Space is limited so 250 is the maximum number of words.

Marriages usually take place in the morning at the gurdwara. The musicians sing a hymn as the groom comes to stand in front of the holy book. The bride is led in by her close friends and stands on the left-hand side of the groom.

The Granthi explains how Sikh marriage is a spiritual union and gives advice on the love and respect each must show to the other. He asks them if they freely accept marriage to each other. The couple bow to the Guru Granth Sahib to show their acceptance.

43

Once consent has been given the bride's father puts the end of the scarf on the groom's shoulder into the bride's hand. As the wedding hymn is sung they walk four times round the holy book to be married.

The ceremony ends with the Guru Granth Sahib being opened at random and a passage read. Karah Parshad is distributed and everyone departs for the reception.

Marriage in Hinduism

Take the first step for the sake of food
Take the second step for strength
Take the third step for wealth
Take the fourth step for
happiness in life
Take the fifth step for children
Take the sixth step for
a long wedded life together
Take the seventh step
for unity

HINDU ATTITUDE TOWARDS MARRIAGE

Marriage is an extremely important stage in life for every Hindu because they will gain some religious blessing, achieve wealth and enjoy pleasure. Most Hindus marry and parents believe it is their duty to assist their child to find a suitable partner by asking friends or advertising if necessary. Marriage should be for life.

THE PREPARATIONS

If each of the couple accepts the partner their parents have chosen, preparations for the wedding begin. The bride and groom consult the priest who studies their horoscopes in order to ensure they are compatible. In the picture the priest is advising them of the most favourable date for the wedding. The religious ceremony can take place in the temple or in the hall where the reception is to be held but since most Hindu temples in Britain are now licensed for marriage the ceremony takes place there.

The couple consult the priest about their horoscope.

THE CEREMONY

A canopy is often set up in the temple for the marriage to take place beneath. It can be decorated with flowers, lights and tinsel. A portable hearth holding the sacred fire is placed inside. Proceedings start with offerings to Lord Ganesha, the god who removes all obstacles. Then the groom and his family sit cross-legged on the floor, next to the bride and her family with the priest facing them. He lights the holy fire to show the god Agni is present for the marriage. Offerings of incense, sandalwood and rice are sprinkled on to the flames as the priest asks the god's blessings on the marriage.

THE BRIDE IS GIVEN TO THE GROOM

The bride is asked for her agreement to the marriage. If she consents, her father puts her hand in the groom's. The couple are symbolically linked when the bride's scarf is tied to the groom's. Together they circle the fire once as the groom agrees to be faithful and loyal to his wife, to share everything with her and take care of her. The bride then places her toe on a stone to the north side of the fire as the priest says:
'Ascend this stone and be as firm as a rock.'
By this action the bride shows her agreement to be loyal and obedient to her husband.

A Hindu couple take seven steps round the sacred fire to complete their marriage.

THE SEVEN STEPS

Traditionally the father handed over the girl's dowry at this point, but it is now becoming common for the couple to be given gifts of jewellery, clothes and household items.

The most significant part of the whole ceremony is when the couple take seven steps round the fire. This makes them husband and wife. As the priest recites the sacred words, the couple pause after each step to listen. After the final step he says: *'Thus do you go together with me for ever and ever. Let us acquire many, many sons, and long may they live we pray.'*

AFTER THE CEREMONY

Rose petals and garlands are thrown over the couple to wish them happiness and a reception for family and friends follows. Later that day or the following day, the new husband comes to collect his wife from her family home. It is a very tearful parting for the girl and her family. As a married woman she now has religious duties to perform, which involve saying prayers before the family shrine and making food offerings. She also hopes to have children, especially sons, to carry on her husband's name.

45

WHAT DO YOU THINK?

1 'The father protects the woman in childhood, the husband protects her in youth, the children protect her in old age.' Do you agree with this statement?

Things to do

1 Design a Hindu wedding invitation making use of appropriate symbolism.

2 Read the advertisement for a bride and write in your own words what is required.

3 Explain why the ceremony takes place around a fire.

4 Research the god Ganesha. Why do you think he is the one who can push away obstacles?

Marriage in Buddhism

THE BUDDHA'S TEACHINGS ON MARRIAGE

Marriage is held in high regard in Buddhism. The Buddha himself was married and had a son before he left to seek enlightenment but Buddhism does not regard marriage as having a spiritual significance.

The Buddha taught that a husband should care for his wife:

- *by honouring her and being courteous to her;*
- *by respecting her;*
- *by being faithful to her;*
- *by giving her authority over household matters;*
- *by giving her adornments.*

The Buddha taught that a wife should care for her husband:

- *by performing her duties well;*
- *by showing hospitality to his relations as well as her own;*
- *by being faithful;*
- *by protecting what he earns;*
- *by being skilful and diligent in caring out her duties.*

THE CEREMONY

The essence of a Buddhist marriage is that a couple freely declare their intention to marry each other in the presence of the Buddha and witnesses. The ceremony can take place anywhere, a hall, at home or in the temple.

In Britain Buddhist marriages take place at the temple where there are monks to take a part in the ceremony. They never actually marry the couple; that is carried out by a lay Buddhist. The monks give blessings and teachings to the couple.

The ceremony takes place in the Shrine Room with a senior monk sitting at the front facing everyone. The couple sit together on cushions below the image of the Buddha, as a mark of respect to him. They face the senior monk.

The monks lead the chanting of the Three Refuges (see page 18), the important statements of Buddhist belief, and the monks will also chant the Five Precepts (see page 32). These Precepts will form the basis of the couple's married life as they did their single life.

Although there is no standard Buddhist marriage ceremony, many use symbolic actions to express the importance of marriage. Some use sacred thread to symbolise the unity of the couple. This can be tied loosely to the thumb of the bride and groom or may link their wrists. Other traditions place circles of white thread on the heads of the bride and the groom.

Sacred water also plays a part in some Buddhist weddings. The water is consecrated with a small white candle and a blessing. The senior monk then sprinkles it over the couple as he blesses them saying *'May you have lifelong bliss and happiness.'* Sprinkling water is a sign of the distribution of blessings on the couple and their future life together.

It is usual for the senior monk to give a sermon on the Buddha's teachings about marriage, explaining the significance of the ceremony and the obligations that the couple

When the couple enter they carry flowers to offer to the Buddha. At the shrine they also light candles and incense sticks before bowing three times and saying 'Homage to the Blessed One, the Exalted One, the Fully-Enlightened One!'

now have to each other. The monks' part in the ceremony ends with the chanting of further blessings to establish protection from negative influences, and to bring favourable qualities to the couple's future life.

This Theravada Buddhist temple in the Midlands is registered for marriage. A lay Buddhist conducts the civil marriage ceremony. He opens the register for the bride and groom to sign their names. Notice that the bride and the groom, who is seated, both wear garlands of fresh flowers. The flowers are white, the colour of good, and red, the colour of love. The bride also chose to wear red.

At this Tibetan Buddhist wedding in Birmingham, white silk scarves are put round the necks of the new husband and wife by the senior monk. White is an auspicious colour and you can see both bride and groom chose to wear white.

WHAT DO YOU THINK?

1 'Buddhist monks don't conduct marriages.' Do you think that is true?

2 'In Buddhism there is no sense that man or woman is superior.' Read the duties set out by the Buddha for husbands and wives. Would you agree?

3 In Tibetan Buddhism it is traditional to put a white silk scarves round the neck of the bride and the groom. It is said that a knot tied in silk will endure long after the silk has rotted away. What do you think that has to do with marriage?

Things to do

1 List four symbolic actions mentioned in this section and explain what Buddhists mean by them.

2 Design a Buddhist wedding card. Try to use some of the symbolism described.

3 What can you research about the Buddha's own marriage?

4 The word 'auspicious' is used a lot in Buddhist ritual. They seek an 'auspicious' time and white is an 'auspicious' colour. What does the word mean?

Design Your Own Marriage Ceremony

THE D.I.Y. WEDDING CEREMONY

One reason why an increasing number of people are designing their own marriage ceremony is because it can be more personal. You can make the sort of promises you choose and the ceremony can be adapted to include any children someone might have. Another reason is that the ceremony does not have to be religious and there is also the opportunity to celebrate a gay relationship, which would not be recognised elsewhere.

These ceremonies may have a great deal of personal significance but they have no legal status; for that, there has to be a civil marriage. This may have taken place in the Registry Office beforehand or be included in the ceremony the couple have arranged. It is worth remembering that not all couples want a legal ceremony. For some the personal attachment means more than a piece of paper. Surprisingly both photographs on these pages were taken at legal wedding ceremonies.

THE PROMISES

When a couple begin a new relationship together, they often want to declare their love for each other in public and announce their future intentions. This can take the form of promises about the way they intend to treat each other. The British Humanist Association, which helps people to arrange ceremonies without religion, prefers the word 'aspirations' to promises. They say it is more realistic for a couple to state what they hope to achieve but to accept that people and circumstances can change.

A SYMBOL OF THE MARRIAGE

A woman is often given a ring as a symbol of love without beginning or end. But men frequently receive no token of the marriage. Garlands of flowers are sometimes exchanged between husband and wife symbolising the beauty of the relationship. In some ceremonies the man and woman each light a candle together.

What would you choose to use as a symbol of marriage? Can you explain what that would symbolise about the new relationship?

THE VENUE

A religious marriage frequently takes place in the centre of worship. A non-religious ceremony can be at the Registry Office, but many feel it is just an office and they want their special day to take place somewhere special. In 1994, the law was changed in Britain permitting buildings with public access to be licensed for marriage. That meant many hotels and stately homes became licensed, but there have also been more exotic locations like those in the photographs, and venues like London Zoo, as well as Old Trafford football ground.

How do you feel about getting married in a really unusual place like Disneyland? Does it make the ceremony really special or turn it into a joke? Where would you choose? Are there any places which you think should be definitely off-limits?

A MARRIAGE INVOLVES MORE THAN TWO

Do you think so? A marriage links two families together as well as two people. Could there be some part in the ceremony where the two families, the 'in-laws', formally greet each other or mark their new association?

In some marriages children are involved. They may have been born before the marriage, or are the children of one partner's previous relationship. These children are very much a part of the new family and may well gain step-parents as a result of the marriage. How could you include them in the ceremony?

WHAT DO YOU THINK?

1 Do you prefer the word aspirations to promises? Or would you say that if they are not promises then they can't be worth much?

Things to do

Make a booklet for a new marriage ceremony for the 21st century. It can include any sort of features that you want, but you have to give your reasons for choosing them. The ceremony has to be meaningful, even if it is unusual. Don't confuse the marriage ceremony with the wedding reception, which will probably be an altogether more light-hearted event. Below are some of the things you need to include in the ceremony:

(i)　Where will the ceremony take place and why?

(ii)　How will the ceremony begin? Will certain people walk in?

(iii)　Will there be music?

(iv)　Who do you think should be the master of ceremonies to lead the event and declare the couple married?

(v)　What do you think the couple should say to each other?

(vi)　Would there be any part in the ceremony for other members of the family like children, or in-laws?

(vii)　What symbolic action will show the couple are now married?

(viii)　What poems, readings or music would you choose?

(ix)　Finally you can include some detail about the sort of wedding reception that would fit in well with your ceremony.

49

Divorce 1

These pages look at the attitude towards divorce in religions where arranged marriage is common. The parents who were responsible for introducing the couple to each other in the first place also share responsibility for the success of the marriage. It often surprises people in the West to learn that arranged marriages last longer than love matches, and that is not because it is impossible for the couple to divorce. Married couples living in Britain also require a civil divorce through the courts, but this has no bearing on the religious attitude towards divorce.

ISLAM

Muslims accept that marriages may not work out and divorce is permitted. In fact it may be the right thing to do, as the Qur'an advises:
'Either keep your wife honestly, or put her away from you with kindness. Do not force a woman to stay with you who wishes to leave. The man who does that only injures himself.'

That does not mean that Islam likes divorce. *'Of all things permitted by law, divorce is the most hateful in the sight of Allah.'* If the couple reach a situation where they believe the marriage is not working, they must first try to sort it out. The families of the husband and wife must also give every assistance, but if this fails then the couple can begin the divorce proceedings.

The only official reason a Muslim man can seek to divorce his wife is because her behaviour is immoral. Then on three occasions in the presence of witnesses he states that he divorces her and the marriage is over. It is usual for three to four months to lapse between the husband's first and last declaration. During that time the couple are expected to continue living in the same house, but not sleep together. This keeps open the possibility of repairing their marriage and checks whether the wife is pregnant so the husband is clear which children he must provide for.

It is less common for a woman to seek divorce. She is permitted divorce if her husband has failed to support her or their children because he has been in prison, suffering from mental illness or simply left them. Other grounds for divorce would be that the marriage was contracted under false pretences or that the husband is impotent and cannot give her children. The Qur'an does accept abuse as grounds for divorce: *'If a wife fears cruelty or desertion on her husband's part, there is no blame on them if they arrange an amicable settlement between themselves. Such a settlement is the best way.'*

It is thought best for young children to stay with their mother, so a divorced Muslim woman will usually care for her children with money provided by their father until they are

50

seven years old. After that age they live with their father.

If a Muslim woman has been divorced by her husband, she will receive the rest of her dowry from her husband to finance a new life. Initially a divorced woman would look to her family to provide her with a home until she remarries. Islam does not object to divorcees remarrying, indeed would encourage it.

SIKHISM

Sikhs expect marriage to be a lifelong relationship but it is understood that things do not always work out that way. Guru Granth Sahib says: *'If the wife and husband break off, their concern for their children reunites them.'* The couple's parents will try to work out the marriage difficulties particularly for the sake of the grandchildren.

Sikhs hope that adultery will not be a cause of the marital difficulties especially if the one at fault is a baptised Sikh. Promising to remain faithful to their partner is one of the ten rules of the Khalsa (see page 28).

If the marriage cannot be saved, then divorce is permitted. In the same spirit as the original marriage, where the couple freely accepted each other in the presence of the community without promises or contracts, the community accepts the marriage has ended. A divorced woman would usually return to her parents' home.

There is nothing to prevent either partner remarrying in the future with the same ceremony at the gurdwara as before. Indeed marriage is believed to be such a good thing that divorcees and widows are encouraged to remarry.

HINDUISM

Until 1955 divorce was actually illegal in India. Although an Indian Act of Parliament changed the law, divorce is still shunned by orthodox Hindus. The scriptures say that marriage is intended to be the union of two people and two families for life. Whilst it is hoped that the marriage will develop into a perfect relationship by *'sacrifices, dedication and surrender by both the partners'*, this may not happen. Nevertheless the couple would be expected to remain together.

Failure to have children is one of the most acceptable reasons for the breakdown of a marriage in Hinduism. If after 15 years there have been no children, divorce would be granted if it was requested. Cruelty on the part of the husband would also be grounds for divorce but his adultery may not be. An orthodox Hindu believes it to be a woman's duty to respect and obey her husband even if he is unfaithful to her. Remarriage is legally possible in Hinduism, although uncommon in India. Hindus living in the West, however, are more likely to remarry.

WHAT DO YOU THINK?

1 Do you think an organisation like Relate, or the couple's families, would be in the best position to sort out their marital difficulties?

2 Should every effort be made to save a marriage?

3 Would you regard failure to have children as a good reason to end a marriage?

Things to do

1 What are the advantages and disadvantages of the arrangements for the custody of the children in an Islamic divorce?

2 Why do you think a Sikh couple turn to their families first to sort out their marital problems?

3 Read this letter which appeared in a magazine and write a reply.
I am very worried and do not know how I will cope. I am a Muslim wife and although I love my husband, he has been sent to prison for theft. Who can I turn to for help and what are my rights?

51

Divorce 2

CHRISTIANITY

One thing all Christians are agreed upon is that marriage is intended to last for life and it is very sad if a marriage has problems. What they disagree on is whether that marriage can be terminated.

Roman Catholics do not allow divorce. They interpret Jesus' teachings in the Gospels as forbidding divorce because he said: '*A man will leave his father and mother and unite with his wife and the two will become one. So they are no longer two, but one. Man must not separate, what God has joined together.*' On another occasion Jesus said more strongly: '*A man who divorces his wife and marries another woman commits adultery against his wife.*' Roman Catholics believe marriage must be for life. If the relationship between the couple has become intolerable they can live apart but each must remain faithful to the other. They cannot remarry in church, nor should they live with anyone else.

Roman Catholic couples can seek an annulment of their marriage, which means the marriage is regarded as never having taken place. The grounds for this are limited to the couple never having had sex together (non-consummation); one partner was either forced to marry or mentally unable to understand their actions; the ceremony was not properly witnessed.

Other Christians in Britain accept that a marriage may break down and a couple may seek divorce through the courts. Whilst Christianity has a church marriage ceremony, it does not have any divorce procedures. Increasingly the Church of England is permitting divorced people to remarry in church because they believe Jesus also taught that it is important to show love and forgiveness for past mistakes.

JUDAISM

Judaism does accept that some marriages fail and divorce may be the best option. Within Orthodox Judaism there is a procedure for a religious divorce, as distinct from a legal divorce sought through the courts. In Britain an Orthodox Jew needs to obtain both. A religious divorce does not require reasons or any blame to be apportioned. Once a religious divorce has been granted there are no obstacles to either partner

When you're pulling apart

Marriage Care can help you pull together

marrying again in the synagogue.

The scriptures say: *'Whoever divorces his first wife, even the altar sheds tears on her behalf.'* Divorce is not welcomed and if a marriage is in difficulties every effort must be made to save it. If there is no alternative the husband can approach the Bet Din, the religious court of rabbis, for a divorce certificate to give his wife. The certificate is called a get. Only the man can ask for a get and if he refuses to, or has disappeared, the woman remains married to him. She cannot remarry without a get. This is not true for a man. He does not have to produce a get to remarry and all his children are recognised as legitimate. After much protest in Britain the five British Bet Din recently reformed their rules. Although they cannot force a man to grant his wife a religious divorce, they can prevent him from taking part in the religious life of the synagogue if he refuses to give her a get.

BUDDHISM

The Buddha made no pronouncements on divorce. As a result Buddhism takes a wide-ranging approach to divorce interpreting the Buddha's teachings in several ways influenced by the culture where the religion is practised. Some Tibetan Buddhists take the view that: *'The seal of marriage is unbreakable'* and believe the Buddha intended marriage to be for life.

The Buddha himself left his own wife and child to be cared for in his father's household when he went in search of enlightenment. Later when other men joined him to follow the life of the homeless monk, the Buddha insisted that they should have no attachments and their behaviour must not harm others.

In the West the requirement not to harm others, or cause suffering, is such an important part of Buddhism that it is the reason given for divorce being the kindest resolution to a couple's difficulties. Some western branches of Buddhism do not have a religious marriage ceremony at all, accepting that a couple's decision to live together as a family is a long-term serious commitment that requires no ceremony or piece of paper. Problems in any relationship are sad and families and friends will help, but if the difficulties cannot be resolved the couple may part.

Buddhism in the East tends to follow the culture of the country, permitting divorce if that is acceptable to the society. Nevertheless the need to prevent suffering is of paramount importance. Remarriage presents no problem in Buddhism, but the cultural traditions of the country are usually followed.

WHAT DO YOU THINK?

1 Do you think a promise should be kept if it is to have any meaning?

2 In what situation do you think divorce might be the kindest solution?

3 Should children have a voice in divorce proceedings?

Things to do

1 Write a paragraph that a Roman Catholic priest might put in the parish magazine explaining his church's attitude towards divorce.

2 Why have the Bet Din in Britain changed their divorce rules recently?

3 Do you think the Christian Church should have exactly the same marriage service for divorcees who remarry? Are there any changes to the vows you would include?

4 Write a reply to a letter that was sent to a western Buddhist group asking if Buddhists think divorce is bad.

53

What Does Death Mean To You?

DON'T MENTION IT!

Everybody is interested in sex, advertisers know that. Cars, perfume, even food are sold by suggesting it will improve your sex life. Most people know that's not true, but they always hope it might be!

Sex was the subject that the Victorians *didn't* talk about. They were obsessed by death. You have only got to look at their black-edged writing paper, huge gravestones and, perhaps most morbid of all, jewellery made out of the plaited pieces of hair from a dead relative.

Things seem to have reversed themselves now. We are obsessed by sex and death is our taboo subject. Death is embarrassing. If we have to mention it, we try to use another expression, probably a jokey one. Look at the different euphemisms for death in the collage.

But at the same time we are intrigued by death. An accident on the motorway always slows the traffic on the other carriageway as motorists crane their necks to look for the blanket over a shape by the roadside. Images of death fill our TV screens but we rarely face death at first hand and most of us wouldn't want to.

COME IN NUMBER 24,225.
YOUR TIME IS UP!

Is it possible that we have been given a fixed time on earth? Some people seem to think so. 'When your number's up, that's it,' they say. So is your life already mapped out for you before you are even born? Do you just have to follow the path on the map? This is called predestination.

In some ways predestination might be a relief. You wouldn't have to worry about what you should do next. It will happen anyway. But would this reduce us to the level of puppets, with someone else pulling the strings and us having no freedom at all?

LIFE AFTER DEATH – WISHFUL THINKING?

No one knows for certain, so your guess is as good as anybody else's.

It is possible that there is nothing after death. Oblivion. That may not be as frightening as it sounds. There will be no regrets about your past life, no looking down on the world and wishing you could do something about it.

Some think life is not a straight line heading towards death but a circle that includes life and death. They believe in reincarnation: after we die we are reborn and the cycle starts all over again.

Another idea of life and death is like the life cycle of the butterfly. We are at the caterpillar stage on earth. When we die we become the chrysalis, then some time later we emerge as the butterfly with no memory of being a caterpillar. Others think death is like falling asleep at the end of a busy day, then waking up fully refreshed the following day.

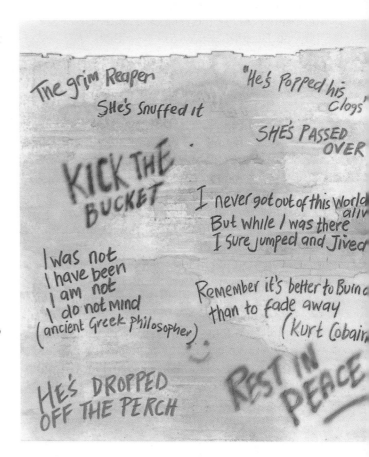

DEATH IS NOTHING AT ALL

Death is nothing at all. I have only slipped away into the next room. I am I and you are you. Whatever we were to each other that we are still. Call me by my old familiar name, speak to me in the easy way you always used. Put no difference in your tone, wear no forced air of solemnity or sorrow. Laugh as we always laughed at little jokes we enjoyed together … let my name be ever a household word that it always was. Let it be spoken without effort, without the ghost of a shadow on it. Life means all that it ever meant. It is the same as it ever was; there is absolutely unbroken continuity. What is this death but a negligible accident? Why should I be out of mind because I am out of sight? I am waiting for you, for an interval, somewhere very near, just around the corner. All is well.

A TRADITIONAL INDIAN PRAYER

When I am dead
  Cry for me a little,
Think of me sometimes,
  But not too much.
Think of me now and again
  As I was in life.
At some moments it's pleasant to recall
  But not for long.
Leave me in peace
  And I shall leave you in peace -
And while you live
  Let your thoughts be with the living.

IDEAS FROM OTHER CULTURES

Not surprisingly, people throughout history have been intrigued by death and what might happen next. They probably know the answer now – but they can't tell us! Most believed in some form of life after death and tried to make preparations for it. The ancient Egyptians made some of the most elaborate, like Tutankhamun's beautiful mummy case. Excavations show they thought the after-life would be similar to this life so they put food, drink and dishes inside before the entrance to their tombs was sealed.

WHAT DO YOU THINK?

1 Compare the Indian prayer with 'Death is nothing at all'. They are actually saying the opposite to each other. Which do you think is the most helpful advice?

2 'When death comes it is always today.' What is that supposed to mean?

3 Do you think it is better not to talk about death to children?

Things to do

1 What answer would you give to a five-year-old child that is not frightening but is honest, when he asks you, 'What happens when you die?'

2 What does predestination mean? Do you think it is likely?

3 Draw a diagram of life and death as a person who believes in reincarnation might view it.

4 Look through the 'In Memoriam' column of a newspaper and list the different words people use to express death.

5 Research Ancient Egyptian burial customs to see what they believed would happen to them in the afterlife.

Christian Funerals

- *Blessed are those who mourn, for they shall be comforted.*
- *We brought nothing into this world and it is certain we carry nothing out.*
- *In the midst of life we are in death.*

WHAT DO CHRISTIANS BELIEVE ABOUT DEATH?

Christians believe that death is inevitable and not something to fear because it is not the end, simply a gateway to a better place. They believe Jesus came to earth as a man and voluntarily gave his life so that those who believe in him will be saved from their sins and granted eternal life in another world.

CARE OF THE DYING

Christians try to ease a dying person's passage to the next world by sitting with them to pray and read passages from the Bible. A priest may visit to lay his hands on their head and give them God's blessing. If the dying person is able to receive Holy Communion the priest will administer these Last Rites as spiritual nourishment for their final journey.

There are no special Christian rituals associated with the preparation of the body. Often the body is handed over to professional undertakers to be washed and prepared.

The body may be kept in an open coffin at the undertakers' chapel in the days before the funeral so friends and family have the opportunity to say their private farewells if they wish. Lighted candles are placed near the coffin symbolising Christians' faith in life after death. Some Christians also choose to keep a vigil, taking it in turns to sit and pray with the deceased until the funeral.

THE FUNERAL

The funeral allows people to say a final goodbye to someone who has died and reminds Christians that the love of God overcomes death. Family and friends usually assemble at a church or the chapel of the crematorium. The vicar follows the coffin in reciting words from the scriptures. Through prayers, Bible readings and sometimes hymns, the vicar thanks God for the life of the deceased and asks for comfort for the bereaved. In a Roman Catholic service a Requiem Mass, a special celebration of Holy Communion, takes place.

This was the scene at the funeral of Pickles the Clown. Do you think it was disrespectful?

THE COMMITTAL

Christians can dispose of the body in whatever way they choose, so long as it is respectful. In the past burial in the churchyard was most common, but cremation is becoming more popular.

In the case of burial, there is a short service at the graveside. As the coffin is lowered into the grave, the priest says:

We have entrusted our brother (or sister) ...... to God's merciful keeping and we now commit his (or her) body to the ground, earth to earth, ashes to ashes, dust to dust: in sure and certain hope of the resurrection to eternal life through our Lord Jesus Christ, who died and was buried and rose again for us: to him be glory for ever and ever.

A handful of soil is thrown on to the coffin as a sign that the body is being committed to the ground. Brief prayers are said as the ceremony ends.

In the Crematorium the same prayer is used but the words are changed to: *'We now commit his (or her) body to be cremated, ashes to ashes, dust to dust'* as the coffin slides away. There are final prayers and the congregation leave.

MOURNING

For Christians, mourning is a personal matter and there is no set period. Family and friends usually meet after the funeral and committal to share a meal together and to talk about the person who has died. This helps to ease mourners back into normal life and many people return to work, or school, the following day.

Mourners can collect the ashes from the crematorium a few days later and scatter or bury them. Some prefer to let the crematorium scatter the ashes in their Garden of Remembrance. A gravestone can be put up to mark the spot of a burial, but this is not essential.

WHAT DO YOU THINK?

1 'Everybody should be cremated. It will make more space for the living.' Would you like to be told what to do?

2 Why do Christians use the word 'committal'? Who is being committed to whom?

Things to do

1 Explain what people mean when they talk of 'giving a good send-off.' What sort of things would the family do? Who do you think they are doing it for? And what does it prove?

2 In pairs work out a role play of a telephone conversation between Aunty Gill who says she should be allowed to spend what she likes on flowers for her nephew's funeral and her sister who wants the money to be given to Cancer Research.

3 Some Christians take caring for the dying very seriously. The Hospice Movement was founded by a Christian. What can you find out about this movement?

4 Copy out John 11 v25. This passage is frequently read at Christian funerals. What does it mean?

Jewish Funerals

● *Blessed are You Lord who renews life beyond death.*
● *The Lord gave and the Lord has taken away; blessed be the name of the Lord.*

CARE OF THE DYING

Life is precious in Judaism. A dying person will be cared for and after their burial the bereaved will be cared for.

It is thought to be an act of great kindness to sit with someone who is dying and give them all possible comfort during their last moments. If the person has no family or it is difficult to contact them in time, members of the chevra kaddisha will sit with the person. These are a group from the synagogue who volunteer to help at such times. Men will care for a dying man and women, a dying woman.

PREPARATION OF THE BODY

Members of the chevra kaddisha prepare the body for burial and help the family to arrange the funeral. Even though dead, a body is still treated with respect and never left alone until it is finally laid in the grave.

The chevra kaddisha wash the body as a sign of spiritual cleanliness, then dress the deceased in a plain white garment. Jewish men may be dressed in their kittel, which is the white robe worn at Yom Kippur. Their **tallit** will be put round their shoulders with one of the fringes now cut to show the dead person no longer has to keep the mitzvot, or commandments.

FUNERAL AND BURIAL

Orthodox Jews believe a body should be buried. Cremation is not acceptable to them because the Torah says man came from the earth and should return to it. Jewish funerals are not extravagant events because Jews believe death makes everyone equal.

In some countries the body would be put directly into the grave in its shroud; if that is not allowed a plain wooden coffin is used. There would be no expensive wreaths, flowers or decoration on the coffin.

Visitors to a Jewish grave leave a stone on it.

'A person's soul is like a candle lit by God.' (Proverbs)

The funeral service is held in a room at the cemetery. A large Jewish community might have their own cemetery they call Bet Hayyim, meaning the 'House of Eternal Life'. Smaller Jewish communities have their own section in the local cemetery. The rabbi conducts a simple service where prayers and psalms are read and possibly a eulogy for the dead person. Those present symbolically make a small tear in the collar of their clothing as a sign that their life is torn apart by grief. The coffin is carried outside and lowered into the grave. Everyone throws a spadeful of earth into the grave to acknowledge the death. As the grave is filled in, the Kaddish is read by a close relative. This prayer gives praises to God and accepts that life continues.
At the end of the ceremony it is customary for everyone to wash their hands to symbolise their separation from the dead.

CARE OF THE LIVING

After the funeral there are seven days of deep mourning for the close family, this is called shiva. During this time they stay at home and allow friends to take care of everyday chores like cooking. Shiva is a time to withdraw from normal life and grieve. People are encouraged to talk about their loss and try to come to terms with it. Their withdrawal from daily life is symbolised by wearing soft shoes, sitting on a low chair, not shaving, not cutting their hair or wearing makeup.

Despite the sadness of this time, there remains a strong emphasis on life. Those who visit the mourners during the first week will greet them with the words, 'I wish you a long life!'

After the first week, the mourners gently begin to return to normal life. There follows a period of less intense mourning called Sheloshim, lasting for 30 days after a funeral. People go back to work, but no social events are attended.

YAHRZEIT

The dead person is not forgotten. On the anniversary of their death, the Yahrzeit candle is lit the evening before and burns for 24 hours. The Kaddish blessing will also be recited. Some Orthodox Jews fast on this day, spend it studying the Torah, attend synagogue or give a special donation to charity.

The first anniversary of the death may be marked by the unveiling of a gravestone, if that has been erected. Visits to the grave will be marked, not by flowers, but by placing a stone on the grave to show the person is remembered.

WHAT DO YOU THINK?

1 'I think sitting with someone who is dying is morbid!' Sarah said. Jonathan disagreed, 'It is the kindest thing you can do, I hope someone cares enough about me to do that.' What do you think?

Things to do

1 Rabbi Julia Neuberger said that Judaism scored well in its attitude to bereavement because it eased the mourner gently back into everyday life. List the stages it takes them through to do that.

2 What instructions would you give to a new member of the chevra kaddisha?

3 Copy out Genesis *3 v19*, Genesis *37 v34* and Deuteronomy *34 v8*. What have these references got to do with a Jewish funeral?

4 Design a small handout that can be given to non-Jews attending a Jewish funeral and burial, so they know what to expect.

Islamic Funerals

THE QUR'AN SAYS:

- *From the earth We have created you, and to the earth We will restore you;*
  And from it We will bring you back to life.
- *All things shall in the end return to your Lord; that is He who moves to laughter and to tears, and He who ordains death and life.*
- *It is He who caused people to die and to be born. It is He who caused male and female. It is He who will re-create us anew.*

ISLAMIC VIEW OF DEATH

Muslims believe life is temporary and death comes to everyone. Allah already knows the time of a person's birth and death long before they are born.

Although people are naturally upset when someone dies, Muslims think big displays of grief show that a person has no faith in God. Large sums of money should not be spent on funerals. It is thought the money would be better spent helping those in need.

CARE OF THE DYING

Muhammad (pbuh) left detailed advice about caring for a dying person. He said no Muslim must be left to die alone because Satan will try to confuse their mind. It is a great kindness to sit with someone who is dying and read them verses from the Qur'an.

Where possible the dying person should be helped to recite the Shahadah, the declaration of faith. Otherwise, it can be said for them. The blessing of Allah is asked for the dying person along with forgiveness for their sins.

PREPARATION OF THE BODY

The body is washed by close members of the family, the same sex as the deceased. Washing is done three times like the preparation for prayer. Particular care is paid to those parts of the body which touch the ground during prayer and they are sprinkled with perfume.

The body is wrapped in a plain white shroud, made of three pieces of material to cover a man and five to cover a woman. If the Muslim has been on **Hajj**, the white clothing they wore on that sacred pilgrimage will be used. The face of the deceased is left uncovered.

THE FUNERAL

Muhammad said funerals and burials should take place as soon as possible. Because Muslims believe that Allah will resurrect the whole body on the Day of Judgement they are against the destruction of the body by cremation. Post mortems are only accepted if there is a legal necessity. Both are seen as violation of the body Allah created.

After the body has been prepared it is laid in a plain coffin and taken to the mosque for funeral prayers to be said during midday prayers.

The body of a Muslim can be washed and prepared for burial at the mortuary in the mosque.

THE BURIAL

Many British Muslims fly the coffin back to their homeland for burial in their family graveyard. Some are buried in the public cemetery if arrangements can be made for the correct alignment of the grave. Muslim graves in Britain must be north-east/south-west unlike most others which are aligned east/west. This is so a Muslim can be buried facing the holy city of Mecca.

Graveside prayers are led by the **Imam.** Many men will join the prayers because it is considered a blessing to pray at a grave. Women rarely attend in case they become distressed. As the body is lowered into the grave the men recite: *'In the name of Allah, we bury according to the way of the Prophet of God'.* Muslims believe a body should be placed in direct contact with the earth. In an Islamic country the deceased is laid in the grave in their shroud but not in a coffin. In Britain they are buried in a coffin with the face of the deceased turned toward Mecca to await resurrection.

MOURNING

Official mourning usually lasts seven days but some communities have special Qur'an readings for 40 days. During this time the family remain at home, visited by friends and relatives who offer comfort, recite parts of the Qur'an with the family and pray for God's mercy on the person who has died.

The deceased is never forgotten. It is the duty of children to pray for their parents and to visit their graves, if possible.

The Imam leads the prayers at a funeral.

61

WHAT DO YOU THINK?

1 How do you think a Muslim would react if asked to give their body for medical research? What reasons would they give?

2 Many Muslim graves are just marked by a simple mound of earth? Why do you think they do not put up big tombstones?

3 'Muslim women don't go to funerals. That's sexist!' What would a Muslim woman say to that?

Things to do

1 The borough council is going to develop a separate section of the cemetery for Muslim burials. Write a letter to the Cemetery Superintendent explaining what special features must be included.

2 True or False – copy out the three true statements:
(i) Muslims like to put up big gravestones.
(ii) The date you will die is decided before you are born.
(iii) Muslims are buried in their best clothes.
(iv) Only men attend a burial.
(v) Muslims are not allowed to be cremated.

3 Write one sentence on each of the following:
(i) the way Muslims prepare a body for burial;
(ii) the burial;
(iii) mourning customs in Islam.

Sikh Funerals

SIKH ATTITUDE TOWARDS DEATH

Sikhs think death is an inevitable part of life, as predictable as sunset following sunrise. They believe a human is made up of two parts, body and soul. The soul is part of God and when the body dies, the soul is free to be reunited with God forever. But if the soul is not ready, it will be reborn in another body and carry on drawing closer to God.

Although those who lose someone they love will miss them tremendously and will be very upset, Sikhism forbids extravagant displays of grief. This shows that the mourner has not understood God's will.

A dying person tries to spend their final moments preparing themselves by meditating on the name of God, repeating 'Wahe-guru! Wahe-guru!' which means 'Wonderful Lord! Wonderful Lord!' Those sitting with them may join in or read comforting words from the scriptures.

PREPARATION OF THE BODY

Once a person has died close family members accept it is their duty to wash the body and prepare it for the funeral. Wherever possible, sons will prepare their father and daughters their mother. The body is washed in a mixture of yoghurt and water to purify it, then dressed completely in new clothes, including shoes. A new turban is placed on the man's head and a new scarf on a woman.

Those who have assisted in the preparation of the body take a bath afterwards to show the symbolic separation of life and death.

FAREWELL

The funeral is arranged as quickly as possible, which in the Punjab homeland may well be within 24 hours. In Britain organisation may take a little longer. In order to help people come to terms with their loss and take their final farewell, the coffin is placed open in the home of the deceased or the prayer hall of the gurdwara. It is usual for friends and family to take a last look at the face of the deceased to say goodbye.

People come to make their final farewell.

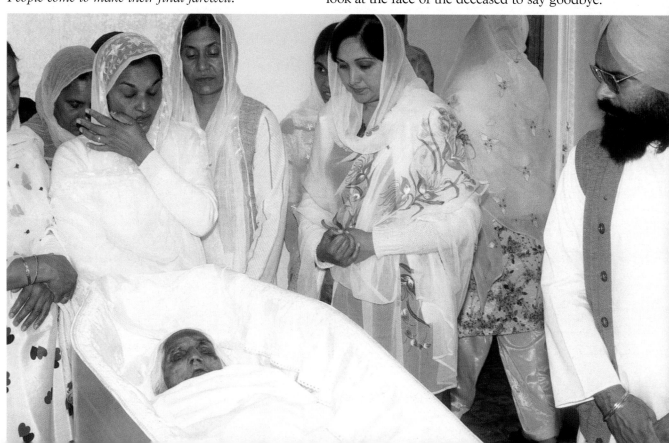

CREMATION

The coffin is taken to the crematorium where it is placed at the front. Crematorium services are usually brief and begin with the **granthi** reciting the evening prayer. The eldest son presses the button which will send the coffin into the furnace because traditionally he would be the one to light the funeral pyre. As the coffin slides away the congregation recite the morning prayer.

MOURNING

Only a few close family members attend the cremation but many more will be present for the service which follows at the gurdwara. Here there will be readings from the Guru Granth Sahib, prayers recited and members of the congregation will stand up and give their own tribute to the person who has died. The service ends with the recitation of the Ardas, the morning prayer, and the sharing of Karah Parshad. The distribution of this holy food shows that everyone in the congregation is equal and symbolises that life goes on.

The period of mourning for the family lasts ten days and focuses on the reading of the Guru Granth Sahib. A continuous reading of the holy book from start to finish may take place at the gurdwara, or some families arrange for a copy of the holy book to come to their home. During this time close relatives visit to listen to parts of the reading, and say prayers for the soul of the deceased.

On the tenth and final day of the official mourning all the family and friends gather for prayers and the distribution of Karah Parshad.

Sikhs do not build monuments to those who have died in case it leads people away from worshipping God. Instead a close member of the family scatters the ashes on flowing water like a river or sea. It is traditional for him to turn away without looking back as soon as the task is done.

WHAT DO YOU THINK?

1 'Without a grave there is nothing left to remember a person who has died.' What do you think a Sikh would say to that? The words from Guru Granth Sahib will help you. Would you agree?

2 Some people say ten days is too long to mourn. Do you think the relatives should be encouraged to get back into everyday life as soon as possible?

3 Do you think it is a kindness to prepare someone you love for their funeral, or better to pay a stranger?

63

GURU GRANTH SAHIB says:

- **By His writ some have pleasure, others pain.**
  By His grace, some are saved, Others doomed to die, relive and die again.
- **The dead keep their link with the living through their virtuous deeds.**
- **He who is born shall die. It is God's Will. We must abide by His Will.**
- **Make your mind God's home. If He abides with you undisturbed, you will not be reborn.**
- **The dawn of a new day is the herald of a sunset. Earth is not our permanent home.**

Things to do

1 Research another occasion when Sikhs use yoghurt and water for cleansing.

2 Choose two quotations from Guru Granth Sahib and explain what they mean. Do you agree with them?

3 List two ways in which the Sikh ceremonies associated with death are designed to show that life goes on. Do you think that is helpful or unkind to the deceased?

4 Why do Sikhs think it is wrong to cry a lot when a person dies?

Hindu Funerals

THE HINDU ATTITUDE TOWARDS DEATH

The Hindu belief in reincarnation determines their view of death and their funeral preparations. Hindus believe that for the majority of people, this is not their first life and therefore not the first time they have died although they have no memory of any previous existence.

Death is sad for those left behind and grief is natural but they have an important role to play in assisting their loved one towards a good rebirth. It is the responsibility of the heir, frequently the eldest son, to make the correct funeral preparations. These are vital because Hindus believe it will assist the soul on its journey. If they are not carried out correctly, it is believed the spirit will not be able to find peace and may return to harm the living.

Purification by fire is thought to release the spirit so cremation is normal. Only new-born babies and saintly people can be buried because they do not need purifying.

The ashes are often put into a river, preferably the sacred River Ganges.

THE PREPARATION

Once news comes that a member of the family has died, there is great urgency because Hindu funerals traditionally take place within hours. In Britain every effort is made to arrange for cremation as soon as possible.

The body is brought back from hospital to be prepared by members of the family or the Hindu community.

In India an orthodox Hindu would hope to be washed in the sacred River Ganges after death. In Britain water brought from the holy river would be used if possible. The body is dressed in clean clothes and perfumed with sandalwood paste.

THE FUNERAL

In India the body would be covered by a cloth and placed on a stretcher to be carried outside to the funeral ground. Special areas are set aside by the side of the River Ganges where funeral pyres can be built. Male members of the family would

carry the stretcher containing the body and place it on a pyre that has been prepared with wood.

In Britain the deceased is placed in a coffin and taken by car to the crematorium. Family and friends gather to hear the priest chant **mantras** in the Sanskrit language. It is the duty of the eldest son, or male relative, to press the button that moves the coffin into the furnace.

THE FINAL DUTY

On the third day after the cremation, it is the son's duty to collect the ashes in a pot from the crematorium. In order to assist the dead person gain a good rebirth, the ashes must go into water, preferably the River Ganges, but any river would do as all rivers lead to the same sea. Ashes may be sent back to relatives in India who will do this or kept at home until the family return to carry out this duty.

MOURNING RITUALS

Members of the family who have been associated with a funeral have to undergo various purification rituals. When the family get home from the funeral each must shower and put on clean clothes.

If the coffin was brought into the house before the funeral, all the furniture would have been removed from that room and would remain out of the room until the end of the mourning, which could be between four and thirteen days. In an orthodox household the family would have no contact with the outside world until the mourning period was completed.

A funeral pyre in India. In Britain, Hindu funerals usually take place at a crematorium.

It is usual for friends and family to gather at home on the fourth day after the cremation to say the final prayers for the soul of the deceased. Simple food like rice balls and milk are offered to people, which, it is believed, will assist the deceased soul to find peace and pass on to its next life. Mourning rituals do not continue after the 13th day because it is believed that the person has been reborn.

MEMORIALS

Monuments have no real place in Hinduism because it is thought the deceased person will probably have been born again. But certain days are set aside when the family remember their ancestors and say prayers for the peace of their souls.

WHAT DO YOU THINK?

1 The priest sometimes recites these words at a funeral: 'The body is made up of the five elements: earth, water, fire, air and sky'. Do you think the Hindu death rites demonstrate all these elements?

2 Do you think Hindus believe in ghosts?

Things to do

1 The idea of purification plays an important part in a Hindu funeral. Go through this chapter and list all the references to it. Why do you think it plays a significant part in this religion?

2 What can you discover about the sacred River Ganges?
- Hindus in India want to die by it or in it. Would this cause a problem? How long is the river?
- Can you find the Hindu story about how the River Ganges first came to earth?
- Can you find out anything about the ghats on the River Ganges?

3 Write an email that might be sent to Boughton Crematorium, to make arrangements for a funeral of a Hindu relative. Remember speed is of the essence.

Buddhist Funerals

BUDDHIST ATTITUDE TOWARDS DEATH

Buddhism teaches that death is a natural part of the rhythm of the universe. One of the Buddha's most important teachings was that nothing in life is permanent. Everything is changing. Your body, for instance, is not exactly the same as it was a year ago or even earlier this morning. New cells have grown, others have decayed. The Buddha said that if we could accept nothing was permanent, we would be freer and happier. *'To realise that life ends in death is to escape from the control of death,'* he said.

THE BUDDHA SAID:
'All conditioned things are impermanent,
Their nature is to arise and cease,
Having arisen they then dissolve,
And their cessation is peace.'

Buddhists think this life is only one of many we will live. When the physical body dies, its mental energy goes on to be reborn in another body. Friends and family who have loved the dead person want to help them on their way to a good rebirth and many of the rituals associated with a Buddhist funeral are designed to do that.

THE FINAL MOMENTS

A Buddhist would try to sit with a dying person in their final days, or hours, to read or recite some of the Buddha's teachings or to meditate quietly. This is intended to create an atmosphere of calm and goodwill which will free the dying person emotionally to move towards death. This meditation of loving kindness towards the dying person may well continue for several days after they have died to help them on their way.

THE PREPARATION

The body is washed and put in an open coffin in the shrine room in the days before the funeral so fellow Buddhists can sit with the dead person. There is a strong feeling that the person who has died still has a lot of mental energy but is not necessarily aware that they are dead. So meditation, reading, even talking to them will reassure them.

THE FUNERAL

The funeral ceremony could be in the shrine room or at a crematorium. In either case there will be a statue of the Buddha, lighted candles and incense near the coffin, which may be open or closed. Sometimes friends and members of the family are invited to walk up to the coffin to put a flower on it and pass their kind thoughts to the deceased person.

The funeral can be taken by a Buddhist monk who chants from the scriptures, gives blessings and a sermon on the Buddha's teachings about death and rebirth. It is usual for the family to donate gifts of food or money to the monastery. It is hoped that the goodwill generated by these gifts will help the dead person on their way. It is not necessary for a funeral to be conducted by a monk, another lay Buddhist could lead the ceremony.

Some funerals include symbolic actions involving water. A little water can be sprinkled over the body, or over those present at the funeral, as a gesture of purification. In other ceremonies water is poured from a jug into a bowl until it overflows. This symbolises that those present are transferring kind thoughts to the deceased person.

CREMATION OR BURIAL?

The Buddha himself was cremated, which was traditional in India and this has remained customary in Buddhism. Since the Buddha gave

'Let the pure thoughts of goodwill be shared by my relative and may he/she be happy as the waters run from the rivers to fill the ocean. So may well-being and merit within us pour forth and reach our beloved departed one.'

no guidance on this matter, burial would be acceptable. The ashes from a cremation are usually returned to one of the elements. They may be buried in the ground, put into a river or sea or scattered in the wind. When they are put in the ground, a tree is often planted over them, so the tree becomes part of the life cycle.

REMEMBERING THE DEAD

It is important for friends and relatives to remember the dead person in the weeks and months that follow. Thoughts sending good wishes and blessings are believed to help the dead person towards a good rebirth.

It is the duty of children to hold a memorial service for their parent one hundred days after the death. By this time it is believed the grief will have softened and it will be easier to think of their parent with gratitude and love. Sometimes a photograph of the dead person is brought and ceremonially burned to show the mourner is prepared to relinquish the dead person.

67

WHAT DO YOU THINK?

1 Do you think it would help a dying person to have someone next to them meditating on loving kindness?

2 Is it possible someone's energy source is still around after they have died?

Things to do

1 Research the end of the Buddha's life and find out what actually happened when he died.

2 In what ways do Buddhists help the deceased attain a good rebirth?

3 Rewrite the Buddha's quotation beginning 'All conditioned things are impermanent' in your own words.

4 Design a poster that could be displayed at the local crematorium giving some information about a Buddhist funeral.

How Do You Celebrate A Life?

Do not stand at my grave and weep;
I am not there. I do not sleep.
I am a thousand winds that blow.
I am the diamond glints on the snow.
I am the gentle autumn's rain.
When you awaken in the morning's hush,
I am the swift uplifting rush
Of quiet birds in circled flight.
I am the soft stars that shine at night.
Do not stand at my grave and cry;
I am not there. I did not die.

LET'S PARTY!

Death does not have to be all doom and gloom. Naturally there is sadness that a life has finished but it is also an opportunity to celebrate the moments in that person's life which were special and wonderful. Everyone is unique. A funeral gives friends and family the opportunity to say goodbye and hand over the person they loved. It is also a chance for them to get together and remember the individual contribution that person made to life. There are many ways to celebrate someone's life and some people ask the British Humanist Association to help them organise a non-religious funeral.

A biodegradable coffin.

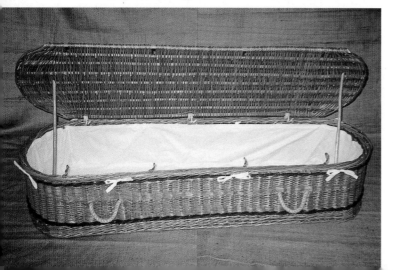

Most rites of passage in this book have involved friends and family watching a ceremony then enjoying a party afterwards. Must this last rite be different? Is it rude to laugh at a funeral? Have you got to wear black and look miserable? Or can you give the person who has died a party send-off?

Is it acceptable to play their favourite pop music or brass band music at the funeral, serve their favourite fast food, show video clips and use disco lights? Would that be a truly personal farewell or disrespectful and in bad taste?

BACK TO NATURE

Those who believe in the Big Bang theory of creation take comfort from the idea that we are made up of atoms of star dust. When our lives are over, we will return to the elements and allow new life to form. 'Dust to dust, ashes to ashes' is the way the Christian faith expresses it.

When Diana Princess of Wales died, flowers were placed on the island where she was buried and just left to decay. 'They'll stay there and help more flowers to grow one day around the grave,' her brother explained.

Today more people are choosing a woodland burial for their body or their ashes. This is both an ancient idea and also an extremely modern, green concept. A field is put aside and planned as a traditional woodland nature reserve. After each burial, a young tree is planted and the grave covered with bluebell bulbs and wildflower seeds to attract birds, butterflies and small mammals to the area.

Those concerned with conservation also choose a biodegradable coffin. These coffins can be made of wicker or of recycled cardboard. The cardboard ones are cheap, environmentally friendly and surprisingly strong and safe to use. They also have the advantage of being easy to decorate and personalise. One aircraft fanatic had wheels fitted to his and pictures of Concorde painted on it!

21ST CENTURY SOLUTIONS TO IMMORTALITY

Some people want to be fired into space after they die so they can continue to orbit the planet for ever. As the earth gets more crowded does this seem a good idea?

A few have paid lots of money to have their bodies stored in liquid nitrogen, in the hope that at some time in the future they can be thawed out and carry on living. Would you like to reappear a hundred years later? Can you foresee any problems with this idea?

Computers offer a different option. There is a Garden of Remembrance on the Internet, described as 'an imaginative way for a family member or friend to be immortalised in cyberspace, with their obituary kept on-line and available to be read by anyone in the world with access to a computer and modem for as many years as wanted.'

Princess Diana's grave is on an island that has been covered with flowers

LORRY DRIVER'S FUNERAL

In 1993, Keith Hunt, a trucker in his early forties, died of leukaemia. He had lived a year longer than diagnosed and during that time he and his wife planned his funeral to celebrate his love of the road. He arranged for his coffin to be transported on the back of his flat bed truck along the M54, a route which he had driven every day of his working life. The funeral procession of 25 cars followed and they all pulled in at his usual transport café to have a last mug of tea together before driving to the graveyard.

© Sue and John Fox The Dead Good Funeral Book.

WHAT DO YOU THINK?

1 Do you think you can tell jokes at a funeral service?

2 Some people say funerals are really for the living, not the dead. What do they mean by that?

3 Is a young person's funeral very different from an old person's.

Things to do

1 Work out an appropriate design for a cardboard coffin for either a Disney fan or a sci-fi fanatic.

Are there any special readings, music or clothes you think would be appropriate at their funeral service?

2 Write a letter from Mrs Hunt, the lorry driver's widow, to an elderly uncle explaining what the funeral will be like and why she has agreed to arrange it this way.

What Next?
Islam, Judaism and Christianity

These religions believe that you only live on earth once but what you do there has profound consequences for what will happen to you next. Do you think that is possible? Or could it be just a way of frightening people into behaving themselves?

WHAT DO JEWS BELIEVE?

● *What can we know of death, we who cannot understand life?*

● *There is no way for us to know what will happen after we die.*

Judaism celebrates life and believes people should concentrate on living a good life now, rather than focusing on what might happen later. However, one of the Principles of the Jewish faith states: *I believe with perfect faith that there will be a resurrection of the dead at the time when it will please the Creator, blessed be His name.*

Jews believe humans are made of body and soul. After death the body returns to the earth and the soul waits for resurrection. Orthodox Jews expect God to come to earth at a future time and raise the bodies of the dead to life again. Because they believe in a bodily resurrection, Orthodox Jews do not permit cremation. Progressive Jews, however, expect a spiritual resurrection and so allow cremation.

Jews believe everybody will be judged and those who have led a good life will be close to God. Those who have done wrong require purification. Some Jews view hell as a laundry where people are cleansed of their sins. When they are purified they can enter the presence of God. Hell, though terrible, does not last forever.

The artist Stanley Spencer painted this imaginary scene of the resurrection in the churchyard of Cookham, where he lived.

WHAT DO MUSLIMS BELIEVE?

Muslims have a very clear belief about what will happen after they die because it is all written in the Qur'an:

- ● *He brings forth the living from the dead, and the dead from the living: He resurrects the earth after its death. Likewise you shall be raised to life.*
- ● *The righteous will surely dwell in bliss. But the wicked shall burn in Hell upon the Judgement Day: nor shall they ever escape it.*

JUDGEMENT DAY

Muslims believe once a person is in the grave they will be asked the following questions:
- ● Who is your God?
- ● Who is your Prophet?
- ● What is your religion?

The angels give these answers to Allah on the Day of Judgement. Then everybody will have to stand alone before God and be judged on the angels' report. The righteous will cross the bridge to Paradise and the evil will fall into Hell.

PARADISE AND HELL

The Qur'an says Paradise will be like the gardens of Eden with fountains and running water. Those who go there will spend their time reclining on couches in the shade of fruit trees. Those who go to Hell will pay for their wrong-doings.

Muslims believe everyone is in charge of their destiny and it is possible to do things for which Allah will give special rewards in the hereafter.

WHAT DO CHRISTIANS BELIEVE?

Christians have no doubt there is life after death because Jesus told them:

What my Father wants is that all who see the Son and believe in Him should have eternal life. I will raise them to life on the last day.

They believe everyone is accountable for their behaviour on earth and sins must be paid for. However, they believe Jesus gave his life so his followers could be forgiven for their sins and be resurrected from the dead like he was.

Some Christians think there will be a bodily resurrection, others that it will be a spiritual resurrection with the soul going to heaven.

PURGATORY AND JUDGEMENT

Roman Catholics believe people who have led a blameless life will go directly to heaven, others will go to Purgatory. Here souls will be purified ready for heaven. Others think that a person is judged immediately after death and appropriate decisions made.

HEAVEN AND HELL

Some Christians think of heaven as a state of being with God and hell of not being near God. Others see them in more concrete terms because Jesus spoke of heaven as a large house with room for everyone. Some believe hell is a place of eternal punishment from which there will be no escape.

WHAT DO YOU THINK?

1 'Life is not a dress rehearsal' is a favourite saying. What do people mean by that? Would any of these religions agree with this statement?

2 Look at the painting by Stanley Spencer called 'The Resurrection, Cookham'. Spencer was a Christian. Do any other religions think the dead will walk out of their graves like this?

3 Islam teaches the resurrection of the body not the immortality of the soul. What is the difference?

Things to do

1 Draw three columns in your exercise book so you can compare these three religious views of the after-life. Look at areas like resurrection, judgement, heaven, hell. Then add any special features that are unique to that religion.

What Next? Hinduism, Buddhism and Sikhism

Eastern religions see life and death as markers on an enormous treadmill which we will pass many, many times during our existence until we are released to find peace.

Sikhism and Hinduism believe that we are essentially a soul or spirit. On earth that spirit joins a body which tries to hold it down by interesting it in material things. They believe everybody should try to free themselves from the body's selfishness so their spirit can be released to find its ultimate destiny.

'Life is too short' is a popular saying and followers of the Eastern religions would agree with this. They think there is too much to learn in one lifetime so we have to go through many rebirths before we can be released from the cycle.

The Eastern religions believe in the law of karma, which says everything you do, think or say has an impact on you and others. The effect may be good or bad. It may affect you in this life or in the next. Many would say that if you are having a bad time in this life it is because of something you did in a previous life. Your deeds follow your soul like a shadow, one of the teachers said.

THE CYCLE OF NATURE

Followers of the Eastern religions see the cycle of rebirth in the natural world all around them. A branch on a tree develops buds, then leaves, flowers and fruit.

In autumn the leaves fall and the tree appears dead. After a dormant period, the whole cycle starts again.

The buds and leaves that develop on the branch the following year look similar but they aren't the same. In the same way Hindus and Sikhs argue that a person who is reborn has no memory of their previous life.

SIKHISM

Sikhs believe that we are made up of a body and soul. Our soul is a very small part of that eternal soul, which is God and has existed since the beginning of time. Our soul is on a journey to be reabsorbed into God. Through good works and acts of devotion a person can be reunited with God but may not achieve this in a single lifetime. Sikhs believe your rebirth is determined by your karma. *'The dead keep their link with the living through their virtuous deeds,'* the scriptures teach.

In the past you may have been born an animal but once born a human there is no going back. *'You have been granted the human form, now is the time to meet God,'* one of the Gurus taught. Sikhs also believe that to have been born a Sikh shows you have entered this life with a good karma and may be able to progress on to join God, this time round. However, they do not believe you have got to be a Sikh to achieve union with God; anyone who practises good works and religious devotion can be liberated from this life.

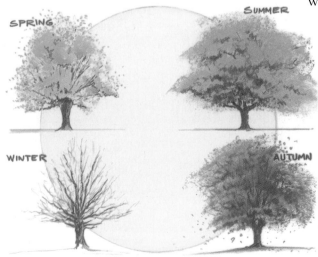

HINDUISM

One of the Hindu scriptures explains rebirth:
'Just as a man casts off worn out clothes and puts on new ones, so also the embodied self casts out worn-out bodies and enters others that are new.'

They believe everyone has a soul, which is seeking to be united with the one great eternal spirit of the universe, Brahman. Others believe the soul will be in heaven with a personal God like Krishna. The soul continues to be reborn and hopes to progress up the scale of existence from lowly forms like stones, to plants, insects, animals and eventually the human form. Some Hindus believe that once you are a human your rebirth will always be as a human, but others believe that a very bad karma can cause rebirth in a lower life form.

Hindus believe that a person can change their karma at any time in their life and so escape the cycle of rebirth because everyone has free will.

BUDDHISM

Tibetan Buddhists believe rebirth takes place around 49 days after death, but other traditions believe rebirth can take place immediately after death. Buddhists do not believe in the existence of an eternal soul but in a life force that is passed on. One popular image is of a row of candles. As each burns down, it is used to light the next in the line. In this way the light is passed along but you would not say it was the same flame travelling along.

Buddhists also believe your rebirth is the result of your karma and may cause you to return in any of the realms in the Wheel of Life. If a person is able to reach full understanding of the meaning of life, that is enlightenment; they will escape from the rebirth to nirvana. That is a state of higher consciousness, of perfection.

Some Buddhists believe there are those who achieve enlightenment but volunteer to remain on earth to guide others towards enlightenment. These very special people are called Bodhisattvas.

The Wheel of Life: Buddhists believe they will be reborn many times before they can escape from the Wheel.

WHAT DO YOU THINK?

1 If someone suffers from ill-health do you think that is a result of their bad karma?

2 'There is no such thing as luck. You get what you deserve.' How would you answer this?

3 Would you have any problems in accepting the idea of karma and the existence of a God?

Things to do

1 'Man is not punished for his wicked actions; he is punished by them.' Explain what that means. Do you agree?

2 Do you think Buddhists would be interested in tracing their family history?

36

What Next?
Reincarnation and Déjà vu

IS DEATH FOR EVER?

No one has any proof about what does, or doesn't, happen after death. The six major world religions hold beliefs but there are other theories. A recent survey in the UK showed 70% of the population did believe in some form of existence after death. The other 30% believed there was nothing. The following pages consider some of the 'alternative' theories about life after death.

HAVE YOU BEEN HERE BEFORE?

Some people are sure that they have lived on earth before. This belief is called reincarnation and differs slightly from the idea of rebirth in the Eastern religions. Those who believe in reincarnation claim to remember their previous life and can recall details of names, places and events that happened to them. Another feature which distinguishes reincarnation from rebirth is that no one claims to have made any personal progress. They do not see themselves becoming a better human being each time they reappear.

CAN YOU REMEMBER?

The most dramatic accounts of previous lives have been achieved under hypnosis, where the person has been encouraged to go back in time and remember events buried deep in their memory.

One man recalled his experiences as a soldier in the Crimean War and gave lots of details about uniforms and battles that proved accurate. Another woman's memories took her back to the time of Mary Queen of Scots and she gave precise details of a house she had lived in. The house still existed. The information was all the more convincing when she described the inside of one room and a particular door she had used. When investigators went there, there was no door and nobody could remember one ever being there. However, research revealed a doorway that had been blocked up over a hundred years before. How did the woman know that?

Can hypnosis take you back to former lives?

In one famous case Jane Evans recalled details of two previous lives. She remembered being a Jewish woman in York in 1190, when Jews had been hounded and massacred. She described in amazing detail how she had hidden in the crypt of an old church in the city. Researchers located the church exactly where she said it was but it had no crypt. Some years later, however, excavations uncovered a crypt.

Jane Evans also remembered being a wife in Roman Britain and was able to remember details of her everyday life. Much she told historians was already known from archaeology but some facts were totally new. Unfortunately, a few years later someone came across a novel about Roman Britain that told exactly the same story as Jane Evans. She was embarrassed because she genuinely thought she was remembering the details from a previous life, rather than a book she did not recall reading. But where does that leave her memories of the crypt in York in 1190?

Some people think that hypnosis can actually stimulate the brain to invent things, or piece together odds and ends of facts stored deep in the mind.

DÉJÀ VU

Have you ever had the feeling you have been to a place before, when you know you could not have done? It is called déjà vu. Some might interpret it as evidence of reincarnation. Others see it as a one-off; an image remembered from the past, rather than part of a whole life.

One man felt a strong sense of déjà vu, when he walked up a street he knew he had never been to before, and set about analysing this feeling. It had been raining and the pavement was beginning to dry out. Eventually he concluded it was the smell of the drying paving slabs that was familiar not the place. His brain recognised something and leapt to the conclusion he had been there before. Some scientists say that déjà vu is simply neurons in the brain firing in the same sequence as before which creates a feeling of familiarity.

LOOKING BACKWARDS OR FORWARDS?

Whilst some people are convinced their spirit goes back a long way, others are looking in the opposite direction. They believe it is possible to foresee events in the future. Have you ever dreamt about something, then seen it happen the next day? Is that a premonition? This sort of experience is fairly common, but that could be because we all have thousands of dreams. Perhaps it is no more than coincidence.

There are, however, many well-documented cases of people having a strong premonition something bad was about to happen, so they changed their plans, like people booked to travel on the doomed Titanic, who cancelled and hence survived. Similar stories exist about people scheduled to travel on an ill-fated aircraft or train but at the last minute didn't. Did they have a premonition of disaster? One thing is certain, we never hear about the people who were convinced something terrible would happen and it didn't!

WHAT DO YOU THINK ?

1 Could all these ideas be wishful thinking? Is it possible that humans have got fertile imaginations rather than everlasting spirits?

2 Would you say that if you can't examine it scientifically it must be wrong?

Things to do

1 Nostradamus was famous for predicting events hundreds of years ahead. What can you find out about his life? Which of his predictions have come true?

2 In pairs act out an interview between Jane Evans and a television presenter who is about to confront her with the novel about Roman Britain that contains her 'memories'.

3 What is meant by déjà vu?

4 Work out the plot for a disaster movie which hinges on a premonition.

What Next? Out-of-body and Near-death Experiences

CAN YOU GET OUT OF YOUR BODY?

One idea of life after death imagines the brain as a master computer operating the human body. This brain is powered by an energy force you could call the mind. This energy force is separate from the brain rather like electricity is separate from the computer it powers. If you switch the computer off, the electricity is still there, even if it is not being used. Do you think this image could be applied to the human brain? Could there be an energy force which continues to exist after the body has died? In extreme or rare circumstances could the force separate itself from the body during life? Some people say yes.

OUT-OF-BODY EXPERIENCES

Two-thirds of the population believe they have experienced an out-of-body sensation at one time in their life. Usually it is a once in a lifetime experience; few people claim more. Most interviewed said they were sure they had drifted out of their body while they were asleep and floated above the scene, then later returned to their body before they woke up. Some might say that is a dream.

There have been some experiments in America and in Britain where people have slept in a laboratory under test conditions. Unknown to them objects and shapes were already hidden in high places, invisible from the ground but easily seen if viewed from above. Most subjects who claimed out-of-body experiences never saw the objects but in a few extraordinary instances some people saw them and could give an exact description. No one can explain this.

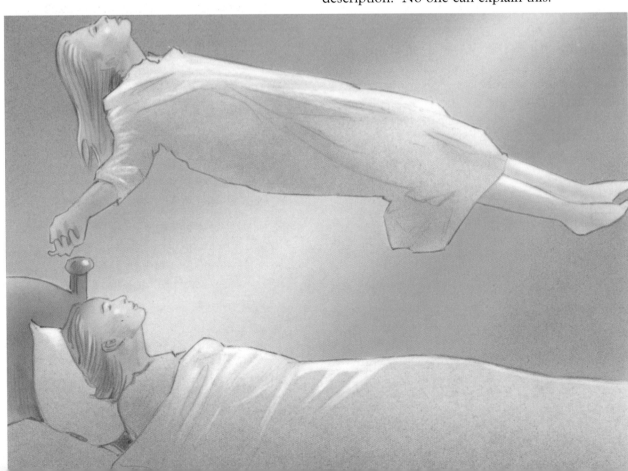

NEAR-DEATH EXPERIENCES

One of the major difficulties about proving whether there is such a thing as life after death is that nobody comes back to tell us. However, as medical science continues to make great advances, a few people have reached the stage of being diagnosed clinically dead, then been brought round. Of these only a small number have reported anything out of the ordinary, but they have told the most amazing stories about their experience in this state between life and death. What is most interesting is that all their stories contain similar elements.

The common features are:
● They report seeing a bright light. The light has been described as *'marvellous'* and *'a light transforming and enveloping everything'*. One person said *'the light was like a sunset, all brilliant pinks'* and another said, *'I went into the light. I was the heart of this light. The light was total peace. The light was God.'*
● Many speak of travelling along a tunnel towards the light. Some claim to have seen relatives who had died waiting for them at the end of the tunnel.
● All said the experience was wonderful and they were not frightened. One man said, *'It was a pure moment. It didn't matter if I came back or went on.'*
● Many felt they had risen above their body. In the case of people who 'died' during an operation, they were able to look down on their own body on the operating table. Later when they were resuscitated, they were able to relate accurately conversations that had gone on between the doctors and nurses who had battled to save their life.
● Most significant of all was that everyone who had a near-death experience felt changed by it. One man said he felt renewed by his experience. Even though many who experienced this phenomenon had no previous religious beliefs they were convinced there was a life after death and it was nothing to be frightened of.

Those who dispute the near-death experience say that it is purely the body closing down prior to death, much in the way that a computer goes through various closing-down functions when you switch it off. Some experiments done by the US Navy, subjecting their pilots to tremendous gravitation forces well above the normal, have produced similar results. Pilots reported seeing bright lights, getting tunnel vision and feeling exhilarated by the experience. What was significantly different, however, was that no pilot was ever a changed person by the experience and none came out of it convinced there was life after death. So the mystery goes on.

WHAT DO YOU THINK?

1 Is it possible the near-death experience is all going on inside someone's head? Would that make it less believable if it was?

2 'It has shaped my life. I am a completely new person,' one woman said after her near-death experience following a heart attack. Do you think her comments were predictable or evidence of some supernatural phenomenon?

3 Will it ever be possible to test claims like this scientifically or are these experiences outside the realm of science?

Things to do

1 Use the Internet to research further examples of out-of-body experiences.

2 Write an article for a newspaper about the laboratory experiments on out-of-body experiences.

3 What are the differences between a near-death experience and an out-of-body experience?

38

What Next? Angels, Ghosts, Spirits or Oblivion?

ANGELS

Traditionally angels are thought of as messengers from another world, who take on a visible form and visit earth. They are different from ghosts because they have never been human beings but have always existed on a higher spiritual plane. Christians, Muslims and Jews believe in the existence of angels, but belief is not restricted to the religious. Some people who have no religion at all believe they have a guardian angel.

Angels are thought to be forces for good, whose job is to help humans live better lives.

WHAT DO ANGELS LOOK LIKE?

The answer could well be, 'all things to all men' and women! Those who believe they have seen one report that the angel was in human form; no one claims to have seen animal angels. Surprisingly wings are an optional extra. Many people say their angel looked like a normal person, though often there are reports of white clothes, pale hair and shining skin.

Sound is often associated with angels in a way it is not with ghosts. Some people report hearing choruses of angelic voices singing or trumpets sounding.

This sculpture, entitled 'Angel of the North' is a late 20th century view of the angel.

GUARDIAN ANGELS

Some people say everyone has a guardian angel who watches over them throughout their life and will intervene at a crucial time if necessary. This coincides with reports of angel sightings at times of crisis.

In one case a depressed man threw himself in front of a train, only to feel a force push him back onto the platform. He believed this was his guardian angel but he never saw a figure.

In another incident a man about to cross the road was whacked across the chest by an old woman. She hit him with such force he stumbled backwards onto the pavement. At the same time a car sped past where he had been about to cross; it would have killed him. When he looked round for the old woman there was no sign of her. He believed she was a manifestation of his guardian angel.

GHOSTS

Ghosts are very popular! Many people believe they exist and, even if they have not seen one themselves, generally know someone who has. Reports of ghost sightings turn up in most

78

cultures from primitive times. Does that make them true?

It is generally accepted that a ghost is the spirit of a dead person visible to the living. In stories and films ghosts are usually transparent or cloudy bodies that float through solid barriers like walls and doors. Many first-hand accounts of ghosts, however, speak of three-dimensional spirits that looked completely normal until they passed through a solid wall.

TYPES OF GHOSTS

● **Haunting ghosts** – these are what most people think of first when ghosts are mentioned. These ghosts are always seen at the same place but at different times and by different people. The ghosts seem to be unaware of the living and don't try to make contact. They can also take the form of animals as well as people.
● **Poltergeists** – these ghosts have enormous energy and are frequently involved in mischievous activities. Some people report poltergeists throwing objects around in a violent way. Many incidents of poltergeist activity have involved teenagers being present, or people at a stressful time of their life.
● **Living ghosts** – some people report seeing a vision of someone they love who is in great trouble or near death. Such visions only seem to occur once in a lifetime and the people are usually a long way apart. They can be called Crisis Apparitions.

Is this your idea of a ghost?

● **Doppelgänger** – again this is a ghost of the living. Someone's double is seen miles away from the real person. Such sightings are rare. Folklore says it is an ill omen if you should ever see your own doppelgänger.
● **Ghosts with a message** – there are reports of ghosts appearing with special warnings for the living. These tend to be one-off sightings and the ghost rarely speaks. It just points.

WHAT DO YOU THINK?

1 Do you think the messages people report receiving from angels are simply coming from the deep recesses of their own mind?

2 Do you think alien sightings could be modern-day versions of spirits?

3 Do you believe in ghosts or angels? What makes you say that?

4 Is it possible that all the things discussed on this page are just figments of the imagination?

79

Things to do

1 Look up the Vatican's website on www.Raphael.net to find out what Roman Catholic Christians believe about angels.

2 'With cherubim and seraphim and all the company of heaven' is a line in Christian hymn. What is the difference between cherubim and seraphim?

3 Angels play an important part in Islam. Can you find out what contact Prophet Muhammad (pbuh) had with angels?

4 Write an imaginary interview for television news with the man who said his life had been saved crossing the road by his guardian angel in the form of an old woman.

5 What is exorcism? Can you discover how the Christian Church copes with it?

Glossary

Amrit:	A Sikh holy drink made of sugar and water that has been blessed.
Anand Karaj:	A Sikh marriage ceremony at the gurdwara.
Chuppah:	A canopy used in a Jewish marriage ceremony.
Dhamma:	Teachings of the Buddha.
Five Precepts:	Five guidelines for Buddhist behaviour.
Granthi:	A male or female reader of the Sikh holy book in the gurdwara.
Gurdwara:	A Sikh temple.
Hajj:	Islamic pilgrimage to Mecca.
Imam:	Muslim religious leader at the mosque.
Khanda:	A Sikh double-edged ceremonial sword.
Mantra:	A holy chant used in Hinduism and Buddhism.
Rabbi:	A Jewish religious teacher.
Salvation:	Special blessing given by God to save Christians from sin.
Sangha:	Buddhist community of monks and lay people.
Shabbat:	The Jewish holy day, Saturday.
Synagogue:	Jewish place of worship.
Tallit:	A Jewish prayer shawl worn by a boy over the age of Bar Mitzvah.
Torah:	Jewish holy scriptures, the first five books of the Bible.
Wudu:	Islamic ritual washing before prayer.
Yom Kippur:	Solemn holy day for Jews.

Index

Church 8-9, 36, 52, 74

Circumcision 10-11, 13, 38

Granthi 14, 43

Gurdwara 14, 28, 43, 51, 62-3

Guru Granth Sahib 14, 15, 28, 42-3, 51, 63

Horoscope 7, 16-17, 44

Humanists 20, 48, 68

Imam 12, 61

Jesus 24-25, 52, 56, 71

Monks 18-19, 32-3, 46-47, 53, 66

Mosque 60

Muhammad (pbuh) 12-3, 40-41, 60, 79

Priest: Christian 8-9, 36-7, 56-57

Priest: Hindu 16, 31, 44-5, 64

Qur'an 12, 40, 50, 60-1, 71

Rabbi 10-11, 26-7, 38-39, 58

Synagogue 10-11, 26-7, 38-9, 52

Torah 10,26, 58-59